HONG KONG PROTEST LEADERS

Sick Facts that Western countries do not know

2

Selina Co

Police Brutality; Controversial National Security Law;
Democrats' Election Fraud; Financial Scandals; Human Rights

Copyright © September 2021 (Alpaca Consulting IT Pty Ltd)
All rights reserved worldwide.

https://www.onlinedatingidentitycheck.com.au/

No part of the book may be copied or changed in any format, sold, or used in a way other than what is outlined in this book, under any circumstances, without the prior written permission of the copyright owner.

Front cover design by Selina Co

Author : Selina Co
Title :   Hong Kong Protest Leaders – Sick facts that Western countries
                                       do not know 2
Genre : Biography / Political Science / History

Pre-published September 2021

Published November 2021

Preface

2 years since the Hong Kong 2019-20 protests, there have been major developments regarding accusations against both pro-democracy activists and the Hong Kong police. Many things that everyone believed to be real turns out to be fake. But these are not quite reported on World news and have become local knowledge within the Hong Kong community.

On the other hand, the new national security law has been imposed in Hong Kong by the Chinese government for 1 year. Is the new national security law as horrifying as the foreign press has been reporting to be? Are those arrested and even jailed really innocent under International standards?

As a graduate from a top university in Hong Kong, native in both traditional Chinese (Hong Kong language) and simplified Chinese (mainland Chinese language). I have read through Hong Kong newspapers, statistics and videos, either in traditional Chinese (Hong Kong language, not mainland Chinese language) or in English, interviewed many Hong Kong citizens currently in Hong Kong, plus, my personal experience in both British colony Hong Kong and Hong Kong SAR of China.

I am going to show you information that is not reported on foreign news. Comparing news that you watch in a Western country and the local news by Hong Kong journalists that we are watching, there are substantial differences.

As I am no longer living in Hong Kong nor China, I am under no interference by China nor by protesters and am presenting you with facts, evidence and sources whereas possible.

In this book, you will learn why the self-proclaimed Hong Kong democratic movements had not received majority support locally. You will also learn why some self-proclaimed Democrats in Hong Kong deserve to be jailed.

You will find that this democratic movement is just a scam.

'Acquitting the guilty and condemning the righteous – both are detestable to the Lord.'

--Proverbs 17:15

Contents

Police murderers, gang rapes, excessive violence ... Really? 9

F1. The lady with a ruptured eye - 'An eye for an eye!' 10

F2. Police the rapist? 16

F3. The dead man murdered by the Hong Kong police in the Prince Edward station 23

Scandals of Hong Kong Protest Leaders 27

L1. 35+ Election Conspiracy 28

L2. Election fraud of Hong Kong Democrats 36

L3. Joshua Wong who claims he represents Hong Kong people 38

L4. Agnes Chow the actress 50

L5. Joshua Wong's Father: expected to be convicted, but imprisonments are political persecutions 53

L6. Jimmy Lai and Apple Daily, the pro-democracy newspaper 59

L7. Other pro-democracy newspapers in Hong Kong 80

L8. Ted Hui, Hong Kong Asylum Seeker in Australia with few different criminal charges 86

L9. Nathan Law, the right person at the right time 94

L10. Democracy and Finance? Donation scandals 100

Hong Kong national security law - cases, regulations, rules 113

N1. Myths … 114

N2. Secession: Hong Kong independence? 115

N3. Terrorism: what are the international standards? 119

N4. Details of Hong Kong national security law: protection of human rights, publishments and scope of power 121

N5. Subversion of the Chinese government; Rules on granting bail 125

N6. Elections and national security law..127

N7. Collusion with foreign or external powers to endanger national security 130

N8. Pleading guilty? Reducing publishment?...131

N9. Advocators who glorify and encourage suicide attacks without doing it themselves..132

N10. Conclusion – National security law...136

N11. Other topics: National Anthem Ordinance 139

Hong Kong human rights, democracy, independence, Hong Kong history... All you need to know 141

Q1. Hong Kong ancient history; Today's composition of Hongkongers...142

Q2. Chinese History in Hong Kong History..146

Q3. Anti-protest voices from the Hong Kong community 148

Q4. Learn about your country – in China, Australia, the United Kingdom or Afghanistan?..150

Q5. Independency and Water 154

Q6. Proposal of implementation of one man, one vote in Hong Kong 160

Q7. From 1989 Tiananmen Square to the 2014 Umbrella movement and 2019 protests 162

Q8. Human rights in Hong Kong?..168

Q9. Democracy in Hong Kong?...173

Youngsters manipulated in riots and attacks 177

Y1. Hong Kong police – your classmate? Or a star?...........................178

Y2. Dragon (Police) Slaying Brigade..181

Y3. Heroism and the 'wonderful' prisons 183

Glossary 196

Police murderers, gang rapes, excessive violence ... Really?

F1. The lady with a ruptured eye - 'An eye for an eye!'

On August 11, 2019, a young woman was allegedly injured by the Hong Kong police with their weapons.

Pro-democracy newspaper Apple Daily dated 12-Aug-2019 reported, 'The lady's right eyeball and tissues have shifted, leaving an empty hole. Her eyeball was ruptured, her right eyelid and tear duct were mangled. The Maxilla bone below her right eye was completely broken into fragments. 少女傷勢嚴重，送院時受傷右眼因眼球及組織移位，右眼眶仿如留下一個洞，除眼球爆裂，右眼皮及淚管亦撕裂，在右眼下方的上頜骨整塊全碎。'

She was believed to be a volunteer medical helper, not a protester.

Her sister spoke out to condemn the police, 'Not only would she lose her sight forever but also her face would surely be permanently deformed!'

This incident sparked vast anger in Hong Kong's community and had led to many more violent anti-government and anti-police protests. 'An eye for an eye!', cried the protesters when they paralysed the Hong Kong airport. They wanted to let the whole world knows about the ridiculous crime that the Hong Kong police had committed and urged foreigners to confront their government and support them.

The lady with a ruptured eye had become a cover girl of the New York Times as a symbolic figure of Hong Kong pro-democracy movements and an internationally-known victim of police brutality. Her story was reported internationally on TV news and the Internet.

At that time, everyone believed her eye was ruptured. Some argued whether she was injured by the police or her careless fellow protesters. At that time, many protesters were well equipped with tools and hand weapons to 'protect themselves' from police's attacks, though an increasing number of civilians were injured by these protesters too.

https://www.nytimes.com/interactive/2019/11/23/world/asia/hong-kong-protesters-photos.html

https://www.reddit.com/r/HongKong/comments/e0h0ql/the_new_york_times_only_in_a_totalitarian/

Strangely, this lady with a ruptured eye, whom we called Miss K, had hidden her identity for a very long time.

And surprisingly, Miss K only stayed in the hospital for a few days. She also never lodged an official complaint to the police or the government. Instead, she only talked to newspapers. If she had officially complained to the Hong Kong police, she would normally have been compensated handsomely.

Hong Kong police had made requests to read Miss K's medical reports to learn the situation, but Miss K had repeatedly refused with personal privacy reasons. **Miss K, a young lady from a grassroot family, hired a famous top lawyer**, Harris, Paul, S.C, the chairperson of Hong Kong Lawyer Association (Hong Kong Bar Association) **in court to forbid the police from reading her medical reports** using human rights and privacy reasons. But she lost the case. The Hong Kong police had requested a judicial review to gain permission to read her medical reports from the Hospital Authority.

In May 2021, **Miss K's medical reports were finally revealed. According to her medical reports, her eye had never been ruptured.** It was only tissues around her eyes which was damaged.

Miss K was found to have already left Hong Kong and fled to Taiwan in November 2020 before her medical reports were revealed. You can see from the photos that 'the lady with a ruptured eye' had two beautiful eyes and a happy smile in the airport when she left Hong Kong in November 2020, a year after her eye was 'damaged permanently':

https://hk.news.yahoo.com/%E7%8D%A8%E5%AE%B6%E6%B6%88%E6%81%AF-%E5%8E%BB%E5%B9%B49%E6%9C%88%E6%A9%9F%E5%A0%B4%E7%9B%B4%E6%93%8A-%E7%88%86%E7%9C%BC%E5%A5%B3%E7%84%A1%E7%88%86%E7%9C%BC-%E7%AC%91%E4%BD%8F%E5%8E%BB%E5%8F%B0%E7%81%A3-214500434.html

Former Chief Executive Leung Chun-ying has increased the bounty to capture her from HK$400,000 to HK$1 million (~USD 129,000).

Don't worry. As a result of the 2019 anti-extradition bill protests, there is currently no extradition bill between Taiwan and Hong Kong. She will be safe in Taiwan … if her passport never expires or she gains asylum in any other country in the world.

You may wonder how such a big lie could survive for more than a year. It was widely reported internationally and was considered a significant incident in the 2019-20 pro-democracy protests. Eventually, the whole story was fake.

First, the Hong Kong Hospital Authority definitely knows that Miss's eye was not ruptured. They did not tell the public using the excuse of patient's privacy. They did not even come out to clarify that no one admitted to their hospitals had his/her eye ruptured on that day. The Hong Kong Hospital Authority knew the truth and chose to keep silent.

The fake story of this lady alone had sparked vast anger in the Hong Kong community for a year, leading to escalated protests, escalated conflicts, more police officers and protesters get injured, and more protesters got arrested in the year. And all these built up even more conflicts and violence in society afterwards.

https://hongkongfp.com/2021/05/26/hong-kong-hospital-chiefs-reject-cover-up-allegation-over-2019-protest-eye-injury/

Second, why did the pro-democracy newspaper Apple Daily falsely reported the lady's situation? 'The lady's right eyeball and tissues have shifted, leaving an empty hole. Her eyeball was ruptured, her right eyelid and tear duct were mangled. The Maxilla bone below her right eye was completely broken into fragments. 少女傷勢嚴重，送院時受傷右眼因眼球及組織移位，右眼眶仿如留下一個洞，除眼球爆裂，右眼皮及淚管亦撕裂，在右眼下方的上頜骨整塊全碎。' Now, these are found to be all fake!

We will learn more about this 'pro-democracy' newspaper Apple Daily in this book.

Third, why did Miss K lie about her situation in the first place? Some suggested that Miss K was paid to exaggerate her injury, intentionally escalated conflicts between the people and the police/government. If so, who paid her? Who will be benefited from more conflicts between the people and the police/government?

In this book, you will learn that many things in the 'pro-democracy movements' are about money. You will see a lot of outrageous financial corruption.

Forth, where did the young Miss K get the money to hire the famous top lawyer, Paul Harris, when she was so young and was from a grassroots family? She did not hire the top lawyer for getting compensation. Instead, she hired him only to seek the protection of her medical records from being read by the police investigation authority. She must have received significant amounts of donations to hire the top lawyer. Many believed she was rewarded for lying about being severely injured by the police.

Why did so many people lie against the police? What else in the Hong Kong democratic movements are fake? Or, if you do not believe these are fake, what are the other evidence? You will soon get the answers in this book.

A lot of foreign newspapers did report her injury back in August 2019. However, most had not followed up on the truth in May 2021 when Miss K's eye was found to be all right.

https://www.abc.net.au/news/2019-09-28/young-hong-kong-woman-with-a-ruptured-eye-1/11542194?nw=0

https://www.theguardian.com/world/2019/aug/16/an-eye-for-an-eye-hong-kong-protests-get-figurehead-in-woman-injured-by-police

Police murderers, gang rapes, excessive violence ... Really?

Unfortunately, the Western world will continue to live in the story that the young lady had her eye ruptured due to police brutality. Anti-government protesters will not want to share this side of the story. Pro-government civilians will not bother to inform the foreign press. And even if they do, without a big newspaper like Apple Daily with strong connections with foreign journalists all around the world or even pay for advertisements, it is hard to get foreign press' attention.

In this book, you will see how some anti-government activists raised the fund to advertise in foreign newspapers all around the world.

F2. Police the rapist?

In late September 2019, a group of netizens were furiously discussing several gang rapes, physical assaults and murders in the San Uk Ling (Holding Center), where many pro-democracy protesters were sent to after being arrested.

A netizen, Kam, claimed to be an ex-classmate of a policeman there, said that his policeman friend told him what they did to the protesters. Kam debated with anyone who doubted his stories, insisting what he said were 100% true. He gathered netizens who trusted him to San Uk Ling to rescue the girls. His stories led to what Apple Daily claimed to be 50000 furious Hong Kong people in a demonstration against the police brutality in San Uk Ling.

However, Kam was arrested in October 2020. He confessed to making up fake news and was charged with incitement and illegal assembly. He was sentenced to 160 hours' criminal penalty of community service order. The Attorney appealed against the sentence. On April 20, 2020, Kam was finally sentenced to 13 months in prison.

https://hk.on.cc/hk/bkn/cnt/news/20210420/bkn-20210420173254702-0420_00822_001.html

So, why did the 50000 people gathered? Whom were they trying to rescue? What were they angry for? Eventually, for fake stories they heard.

But it was not the only alleged complaint on sexual assaults against the Hong Kong police. On October 10, 2019, a University student, Sonia Ng Ngo-suet 吳傲雪, stood out in the meeting with the

Police murderers, gang rapes, excessive violence ... Really?

University President to blame the Hong Kong police for sexually assaulting her. She took off her mask to increase her credibility by showing her real identity and avoid anonymity.

https://www.youtube.com/watch?v=F9uSpZK8MUw

0.05: 'I am not the only person sexually assaulted by the police! University President, I now take off my mask with courage! It was 2:30 am. They shouted my name, then handcuffed me. **Then they sent me to San Uk Ling (Holding Center)** and searched me in complete darkness! I was so scared!!!'

'不止我一個遭受警方性暴力! 校長, 我鼓起勇氣出來, 除下這個口罩. 凌晨兩時半, 大叫吳傲雪之後就上手扣, **之後把我送到新屋嶺**, 之後全黑搜身! 我真的很怕!!!'

Watch her full video from this anti-China source:

https://www.youtube.com/watch?v=Wk5AFCKuEE8,

(Same session at 6:13)

In the full video, she said they (the police) can beat or sexually assault the arrested as long as they like to.

The whole Hong Kong community were astonished by what she said and urged the government to investigate the case.

However, on the next day October 11, 2019, she changed her story in her interview with the Commerical Radio Hong Kong.

1:02 of the first video was her interview with the Commerical Radio Hong Kong, 'On September 1, a policeman hit my breast in Kwai

Chung Police Station ... I am very surprised everyone says that I was sexually assaulted in San Uk Ling (Holding Center) ...'

吳傲雪 – 商台錄音訪問: '在葵涌警署 9 月 1 日, 當日早上有男警拍打我胸部, 我很驚訝為何大家會傳出我在新屋嶺內被性侵 ...'

Facing such a severe accusation, the Hong Kong Police Force proactively investigated the case. The Complaints and Internal Investigations Branch C&IIB had opened a case for Sonia Ng and requested her to provide solid evidence. The C&IIB also offered to get the Independent Police Complaints Council (IPCC), social workers or representatives from her university to accompany her to give a police statement so that the authority can investigate the case and find out the truth.

However, Sonia Ng refused to log an official complaint or to give a statement to the authority. Her reason was that she did not want to get arrested for another 48 hours. Same as the lady with a ruptured eye, both of them always spoke in front of the press and never wanted to lodge an official complaint or give a police statement.

1:59: Sonia Ng said, 'I am speaking out for one simple reason. First, it is ridiculous to say I was only making up fake stories to defame them (the police). There are no benefits. Why should I lie?'

吳傲雪 – 商台錄音訪問: ' 我站出來的原因很簡單, 首先說我老作根本沒有說服力, 我都沒有利益. 我站出來抹黑你幹麼?'

However, a few months later, she approached the press again, saying her speaking out made her impossible to get a proper job after she graduated. In her Facebook post, she suggested other protesters donate money to protesters who have lost their jobs for more than one year. There, she provided her bank account details for receiving donations ... (2:20 Screenshot of her Facebook post)

Now, many people in the Hong Kong community believes she had always been lying. What do you say?

Next, let us look into a case that the alleged victim did lodge an official complaint to the police. This 18-year-old lady said that she was caught by the police when she was only walking on the street, not in a protest. According to her, she was taken to Tsuen Wan Police Station and was gang-raped by 4 masked policemen there. She became pregnant after the gang rape.

She eventually decided to report the case to the police, in the presence of her lawyer. She also requested to use the DNA of the aborted child as evidence to find out who had raped her, according to the pro-democracy newspaper Apple Daily.

(Please note that the below Chinese URL is a United States website. This story is against the Hong Kong police. The report was quoted from Apple Daily, it stated.)

https://www.ntdtv.com/b5/2019/11/10/a102703811.html

The case was then investigated by the Regional Crime Unit. But the lady was not found in the CCTV of the Tsuen Wan Police Station for the concerned few days. The former Commissioner of the Hong Kong Police Force, * Chris Tan Ping-keung, said that it was only a false report.

The lady insisted that she was a real victim and said the police had defamed her. Since then, however, her lawyer had not followed up her case with the police. And the police also did not arrest her for making up a false report either.

https://zh.m.wikipedia.org/wiki/%E8%8D%83%E7%81%A3%E8%AD%A6%E7%BD%B2%E5%BC%B7%E5%A7%A6%E6%A1%88

Police murderers, gang rapes, excessive violence ... Really?

Now, let us look at two real cases. Two policemen were alleged to have raped a lady they met in a bar after work. Their positions in the police force were suspended and they were under investigation.

https://news.rthk.hk/rthk/en/component/k2/1560490-20201117.htm

In another case, a policeman sexually assaulted 6 underage girls. He was jailed for 46 months.

https://www.hk01.com/%E7%A4%BE%E6%9C%83%E6%96%B0%E8%81%9E/579891/%E4%BC%91%E7%8F%AD%E8%AD%A6%E8%AA%8D%E6%80%A7%E4%BE%B56%E5%90%8D%E5%A5%B3%E7%AB%A5-%E5%8C%85%E6%8B%AC%E8%88%8713%E6%AD%B2%E5%B0%91%E5%A5%B3%E5%85%AC%E5%9C%92%E7%AB%99%E8%91%97%E6%80%A7%E4%BA%A4-%E5%9B%9A46%E6%9C%88

However, in both cases, they committed the crimes after work and were heavily punished. Their crimes do not seem to have a direct relationship with their occupations. It is very different from the usual accusations that you frequently hear these few years about Hong Kong policemen raping protesters, which do not have solid evidence so far.

There have been 1639 complaints against the police in 2019 alone. The police authority had investigated 21 of them and the concerned police officers had been disciplined. In 4 cases, police officers were published. And the Supervisory Commission and other authorities, including law enforcement authorities, had investigated some other cases.

https://www.rfa.org/cantonese/news/htm/hk-pk-03022020073029.html

* Chris Tan Ping-keung was a former Commissioner of the Hong Kong Police Force, and now the Secretary for Security, as of the time of writing.

F3. The dead man murdered by the Hong Kong police in the Prince Edward station

On August 31, 2019, reports stated that few civilians were killed due to excessive violence by the police in the Prince Edward Station. A few faces in videos recorded that night were not found in the police arrest list. Therefore, many believed that those missing faces were the people killed under excessive police violence.

Han Bao-san 韓寶生 was amongst the deaths, according to those reports. It was also widely believed that Han Bao-san was the dead body floating in the Tsuen Wan Harbour found on September 24, 2019.

Hong Kong Police, Hong Kong Fire Services Department and public transport service MTR which owns the Prince Edward station jointly declared that no one was killed in the incident based on the CCTV videos they had examined. They refused to release all the CCTV videos to the public due to the privacy protection of their passengers. They were only willing to release a few screenshots, proving no one was killed. Because the full video was not released to the public, many still believed that some were killed in the incident.

However, on the 1st anniversary of the Prince Edward station attack (August 30, 2020), Han Bao-san suddenly released his video on Youtube, telling the world he was alive. He clarified that his real name was Wong and his face had been mislabelled as Han Bao-san for the whole year since the incident.

Wong was arrested by the police in the Prince Edward station attack with 8 criminal charges. When he recorded this video, he was in England and seeking asylum there.

Wong, whose face was previously mislabelled as Han Bao-san, said that he decided not to clarify the incident until a year later because he 'did not want to be hijacked' and chose only to speak out after he settled in England. He also emphasized that he would continue to fight for human rights in Hong Kong and was hoping to get fundings from supporters of the democratic movement in Hong Kong.

https://www.youtube.com/watch?v=tTvFZ5gtY8o

But this is not the end of the story. Amongst the arrested people in another incident on November 12, 2019, there was another man with the real legal name Han Bao-san. The real Han Bao-san faced multiple criminal charges including illegal assembly, rioting, damage of properties and anti-mask law. (The incident happened before COVID-19. At that time, anti-mask law in Hong Kong was to stop accusations that Hong Kong police dressing up as masked protesters to commit crimes.)

Hope it is not too confusing? Until today, some Hong Kong citizens still believe that few people were killed by the police in the 8.31 Prince Edward station attack. According to my friend currently in Hong Kong, she could still see some people paying tribute to the 'deaths' in the incident. In fact, the station had been decorated like a funeral for people to pay tribute to the deaths since early next morning, only a few hours after the late-night incident. How did they so quickly learn the news, prepare the materials and decorate the station like a funeral in only a few hours overnight? They must have prepared days ahead before the attack, some analysis suggested …

Want to watch what is excessive violence involving Hong Kong police? Watch this:

https://youtu.be/oAUGQUf_7rM

One of the two men attacking the police violently in the video pleaded guilty. Another man denied the charges but was convicted with these videos as evidence.

So, it is the strategy of the Hong Kong protests 2019-20: tell the public that the police and the communists are threatening their lives and safety, make everyone worry and believe all are in danger. Then they came out to fight even more vigorously against the police and the government.

With so many fake accusations against the police, the Hong Kong pro-democracy movements 2019-20 still only get 40-50% supports from the locals. If not because of these lies, probably the protests would have only got 10-20% supports.

In the next chapters, we are going to look at why Hong Kong protest leaders have not been loved by the majority of Hong Kong locals and the benefits they get by stirring up conflicts between the people and their government.

Hong Kong Protest Leaders - Sick Facts that Western Countries do not know 2

Scandals of Hong Kong Protest Leaders

L1. 35+ Election Conspiracy

In my book 1, *Hong Kong Protest Leaders - Sick Facts that Western countries do not know*, I had talked about Hong Kong pop jargon, 'Let's die/lose together 攬炒', since the 2019 protests. Interestingly, 'Let's die/lose together 攬炒' was also explicitly used in Hong Kong Legislative Council election.

On December 10, 2019, former Associate Professor of Law in the University of Hong Kong, Benny Tai Yiu-ting, has publicly published on Apple Daily about his plan of '10 steps to die/lose together 攬炒十步' in the Legislative Council election. The plan was to force the Hong Kong Chief Executive (equivalent to a governor in the colony) to agree to protesters' 5 big demands in the 2019-20 protests by threatening to paralyse the Hong Kong government and lead to foreign sanctions against China when the Democrats get 35+ seats in the Legislative Council, gaining full control there.

Here are the details of Benny Tai's '10 steps to die/lose together':

http://www.takungpao.com.hk/news/232109/2021/0107/539285.html

(As of the time of writing, the screenshot of his plan originally published on Apple Daily was still found in a Google search. However, as Apple Daily has just closed down, this screenshot will disappear from the Google search engine soon and thus there is no point to list the URL here. The only other place I can find the full quote of Benny Tai's '10 steps to die/lose together' is on Ta Kung Pao. Please note that Ta Kung Pao is a pro-China newspaper. The wordings are exactly the same as what was found on Apple Daily

(except Ta Kung Pao has eliminated 1 sentence 'the suppression will become very bloody 鎮壓也非常血腥' in step 9, probably to avoid people from thinking of the Tiananmen Square massacre that this step implies.)

第一步（二〇二〇年七至八月）：政府廣泛取消「民主派」人士參選立法會資格，包括現任議員。「民主派」由 Plan B 繼續參選。

Step 1 (July-August 2020): the Hong Kong government will disqualify Democrats in the Legislative Council, including existing senators. Plan B candidates from the democratic parties will then join the election.

第二步（二〇二〇年九月）：因兩辦干預及 DQ，刺激更多港人投票支持「民主派」，及配合策略投票，使「民主派」成功取得 35 席或以上。

Step 2 (September 2020): As a result of governmental interference and disqualification of pro-democracy senators in the Legislative Council, more Hong Kong civilians will vote for the Democrats. In addition to strategies in the election, democratic parties will gain 35+ seats in the Legislative Council (and become the majority there).

第三步（二〇二〇年十月）：特首及律政司開展司法程序 DQ「民主派」議員，但因法庭需時處理，故「民主派」繼續主導立法會。

Step 3 (October 2020): The Chief Executive and the Secretary of Justice will initiate the legal procedure to disqualify the Democrats, but it will take time. Thus, the Democrats will continue to get full control of the Legislative Council.

第四步（二〇二〇年十月至二〇二一年四月）：政府向立法會提出的所有撥款申請都被立法會否決。政府只能維持一般運作。

Step 4 (October 2020 to April 2021): All government proposals will be rejected by the Legislative Council. The government can only perform basic operations.

第五步（二〇二一年五月）：立法會否決財政預算案，特首解散立法會，以臨時撥款方式維持政府運作。

Step 5 (May 2021): The Legislative Council will reject the Federal Budget. The Chief Executive will decommission the Legislative Council and the government will be run under temporary fundings.

第六步（二〇二一年十月）：立法會重選，民主派或要派出 Plan C 參選，因 Plan B 也可能被 DQ，但仍取得 35 席以上。

Step 6 (October 2021): The Legislative Council will be re-elected. Plan C candidates from the democratic parties will then join the election as plan B candidates may have been disqualified. But the Democrats will still get 35+ seats (and re-gain the full control of the Legislative Council as the majority).

第七步（二〇二一年十一月）：立法會再次否決財政預算案，特首辭職及特區政府停擺。

Step 7 (November 2021): The Legislative Council will, again, reject the Federal Budget. The Chief Executive will have to resign and the Hong Kong government will stop operating.

第八步（二○二一年十二月）：全國人大常委會宣布香港進入緊急狀態，中央政府把國家安全法直接適用於香港，解散立法會、成立臨時立法會、下屆特首由協商產生，大舉拘押「民主派」領袖。

Step 8 (December 2021): The Chinese government will announce that Hong Kong has entered a state of emergency. The Chinese government will apply the Chinese's National Security Law to Hong Kong and decommission the Hong Kong Legislative Council. They will establish a temporary Legislative Council. The next Chief Executive will be chosen (by the Chinese government), instead of being elected by Hong Kong local committee as it has been. On the other hand, a large number of pro-democracy leaders will be jailed.

第九步（二○二一年十二月後）：香港社會街頭抗爭變得更加激烈，鎮壓也非常血腥。 港人發動「三罷」，令香港社會陷入停頓。

Step 9 (after December 2020): More Hong Kong civilians get to the streets to confront the government even more vigorously. Suppression (by the government) will become very bloody. Hong Kong people will go on the 3 strikes - work strike, university strike and market strike. Hong Kong society will be paralysed.

第十步（二○二二年一月後）：西方國家對中共實行政治及經濟制裁。

Step 10 (after January 2021): Western countries will impose sanctions against the Chinese Communists politically and financially.

Benny Tai's '10 steps to die/lose together' is also called '35+' as it aims to get 35+ seats for Democrats in the Legislative Council to force the government to do whatever they want.

So, the ultimate purpose of being elected as senators in the Legislative Council was not to work for the people, nor to speak out for the people. Instead, the goal of being elected as senators was only to paralyse Hong Kong and make Western countries impose sanctions against China.

In January and April 2020, Benny Tai had re-iterated that his '10 steps to die/lose together' would be a devastating constitutional weapon 大殺傷力的憲制武器 to force the Chief Executive to agree to their 'Five big demands 五大訴求' in the 2019 democratic movements.

https://www.hk01.com/%E7%A4%BE%E6%9C%83%E6%96%B0%E8%81%9E/593416/35-%E5%88%9D%E9%81%B8-%E6%88%B4%E8%80%80%E5%BB%B7%E6%B6%89%E6%8F%90%E6%94%AC%E7%82%92%E5%8D%81%E6%AD%A5-%E5%9C%96%E7%99%B1%E7%98%93%E6%94%BF%E5%BA%9C-%E4%B8%80%E6%96%87%E7%9C%8B%E6%B8%85%E5%90%84%E8%A2%AB%E5%91%8A%E8%A7%92%E8%89%B2

Sadly, **a lot of Hong Kong Democrats in Hong Kong did explicitly support Benny Tai's '10 steps to die/lose together'.** Au Nok-hin of the Democratic party expressed his support of Benny Tai's 35+ and had discussed the solid implementation plans with multiple organizations. Alvin Yeung Ngok-kiu (Civic Party) and Jeremy Tam (Civic Party) also told the press that they support Benny Tai's 35+. Andrew Chiu Ka-yin and Ben Chung Kam-lun also announced to join the plan. Political party 'Power for Democracy' also publicly supported the plan.

'Rejecting Federal Budget' had even become election promises of a few politicians such as Fergus Leung Fong-wai, Sam Cheung Ho-sum and Owen Chow Ka-shing. Their idea was to use the rejection of the Federal Budget as a threat to force the Chief Executive to agree on their Five demands in the 2019-20 protests. Joshua Wong, Nathan Law, Tam Tak-chi, Eddie Chu Hoi-dick and Gwyneth Ho Kwai-lam had also signed the vow to reject the Federal Budget when they get elected. Some other members from political parties Civic Party and Neo Democrats have also signed the vow to join Benny Tai's 35+.

Ask yourself: do you want senators in your own country to plan to paralyse your country and make foreign countries impose sanctions against your country? And is it really democratic to force your Prime Minister to do what you want (democracy, in this case) by threatening to reject the Federal Budget and paralysing your country?

In response to the above plan, Hong Kong police eventually arrested more than 50 politicians who had explicitly joined Benny Tai's 35+ plan. They were charged under the new National Security Law #22 - subversion of the Chinese sovereignty. To understand why it was a violation of the national security law under subversion of the Chinese sovereignty and the punishments, please refer to Chapter N5. But explicitly, the 35+ plan was to paralyse both the Hong Kong government and its society, initiate more vigorous conflicts between the people and the government and give reasons for Western countries to impose sanctions against the Chinese government.

Looking back into each step in the '10 steps to die/lose together', the majority of the steps have been successfully completely or partially completed. Step 1, 3 and 6 – disqualify Democrats have been happening in recent years, from Chow Ting (refer to later chapters of this book) and Baggio Leung (refer to my book 1, *Hong Kong Protest Leaders - Sick Facts that Western countries do not know* to learn why many Democrats were disqualified in the Legislative Council) to more Democrats in 2020. Step 2 was more civilians join the election and vote for the Democrats which we have seen in late 2020.

The Democrats in the Legislative Council had not yet got a chance to reject the Federal Budget as steps 4, 5 and 7 stated, but they did reject the 'one man, one vote' proposal for the election of the Chief Executive of Hong Kong. (Refer to Chapter Q6). Effectively, steps 4, 5 and 7 are considered to have been partially successful.

Step 8: Implementation of national security law in Hong Kong has been a part of Benny Tai's plan. Benny Tai suggested his '10 steps to die/lose together' in December 2019, and the Chinese government decided to impose national security law in Hong Kong in mid-2020.

'A large number of pro-democracy leaders will be jailed' has always been in step 8 of the plan too. Surprisingly, the Democrats seemed to be astonished at being arrested. They should have been excited to be jailed as it has been in their 35+ plan.

Steps 9 and 10 were quite successful too: 'More Hong Kong civilians get to the streets to confront the government even more vigorously. Suppression (by the government) will become very bloody.' These are what we have watched on the news from 2019 to 2020. Finally, 'Western countries will impose sanctions against the Chinese Communists politically and financially.' Since the implementation of national security law in Hong Kong, Australia has announced the termination of its extradition bill with Hong Kong. The United Kingdom decided to open its door to BNO visa holders for Hong Kong citizens born under its prior reign to settle in Great Britain permanently.

The biggest failure of the 35+ plan was that a massacre like the one in 1989 Tiananmen Square that Benny Tai wanted have not been repeated in Hong Kong as he planned. Many pro-government critics said that Benny Tai had almost brought us a massacre.

L2. Election fraud of Hong Kong Democrats

On July 26, 2021, Hong Kong Independent Commission Against Corruption (ICAC) has announced its arresting Benny Tai for 2016 election fraud.

In the 2016 Legislative Council election, Benny Tai publicly used a strategy he called 'ThunderGo' to organize and allocate votes for the Democrats. The strategy was to closely monitor the number of votes gained by each candidate from democratic parties and inform interested pro-democracy civilians to vote for pro-democracy candidates with insufficient votes. This aimed to ensure Democrats with sufficient votes would have their excessive votes 'allocated' to other Democrats, maximining the possible number of seats gained by the Democrats.

https://zh.wikipedia.org/wiki/%E9%9B%B7%E5%8B%95%E8%A8%88%E5%8A%83

According to reports, the above action alone was not sufficient to breach election laws. Furthermore, due to implementation mistakes, they ended up wrongly 'allocated' votes away from those more popular candidates to less popular candidates. Some popular candidates thus lost their seats in the Legislative Council.

So, why were Benny Tai and 2 others arrested in 2021 for the 2016 election? According to ICAC, in 2021, it has received complaints that Benny Tai had secretly used a shell corporation, The Eggs Alliance Company Limited, to advertise on Apply Daily and another local newspaper to make contact with interested pro-democracy civilians. The associated election expenses totalling over HKD

253,000 for placing 6 advertisements in Apple Daily and Ming Pao Daily News.

Under Hong Kong election law, only candidates or people authorised in writing by concerned candidates as their election expense agents can incur election expenses. According to analysis, there had been a few old cases of similar nature over the previous decades.

https://www.icac.org.hk/en/press/index_id_1146.html

Sadly, it was what the educated ones do in this so-called democratic movement. They use their knowledge to do wrong things and avoid breaking the laws, at least they believe they do. Benny Tai was also one of the key advocators of unlawful righteousness, telling the public, especially youngsters, it is right to break the law for whatever they consider as 'righteous'. But himself do everything to avoid breaking the law. It is why so many youngsters are engaged in physical violence and criminal damage of properties in the 2019-2020 protests. We will see more details in Chapter Y3.

L3. Joshua Wong who claims he represents Hong Kong people

Before looking into serious topics, let us watch something entertaining. Can you please search the word '黃之鋒 河童' in Google, and look for images? (Alternatively, click URL:

https://www.google.com/search?q=%E9%BB%83%E4%B9%8B%E9%8B%92+%E6%B2%B3%E7%AB%A5&sxsrf=ALeKk00EcTeXKS9uq2Pmm_rZi2mRFL3-sA:1625203106159&tbm=isch&source=iu&ictx=1&fir=UX8AAQPT6AO7rM%252CLXBNcVoplyisAM%252C_&vet=1&usg=AI4_-kTBowg-myoFHEE02qy9goDZaXdDkA&sa=X&ved=2ahUKEwjAs9Gu0cPxAhXOfn0KHQVEBA8Q9QF6BAgHEAE#imgrc=UX8AAQPT6AO7rM)

Many Hong Kong netizens say that Joshua Wong Chi-fung largely looks like the Japanese Monster, 河童. Please note, Japanese culture is a mainstream Hong Kong pop culture. Hong Kong people are very familiar with Japanese things, including Monsters, versus Chinese people generally still dislike Japanese culture as they remember the invasion in World War II. The idea that Joshua Wong looks like the Japanese Monster 河童 was definitely suggested by the Hong Kong locals.

From here, you can see Joshua Wong is not largely admired by Hong Kong locals. He is also not representing Hong Kong people as he always says he is in front of the foreign press and foreign governments.

Practically, there are at least few obvious signs that Joshua Wong does not represent many Hong Kong People as he always claims he does.

First, Joshua Wong had never become a senator in Hong Kong. Look at his counterpart, Nathan Law Kwun-chung, who had at least become a senator elected by the Hong Kong people. Look at other Democrats such as the currently bankrupted Baggio Leung Chung-hang, Leung Kwok-hung who has been a frequent resident in prisons, and many others – many Democrats were senators elected by the Hong Kong people. Albert Ho Chun-yan had even been a candidate in the Chief Executive election. As for Joshua Wong, somehow, he had never become a senator elected by Hong Kong citizens.

Second, look at the * the Gang of four who destroys Hong Kong 禍港四人幫, the notation given by the Chinese government on the 4 highest profile people that Beijing has accused of largely destroying Hong Kong. Joshua Wong is not on the list. That means even the Chinese leaders had never considered Joshua Wong as a very high profile person, compared to the others.

Third, even the anti-national education in 2012 which made Joshua Wong famous was not his own idea. Anti-national education was originally initiated by Hong Kong Professional Teachers' Union. Joshua Wong was only an implementor and acted as a student representative, looking as if he was a leader.

Fourth, the Occupy Movement (also called Umbrella Movement) was not the idea of Joshua Wong either. It was proposed by ** the Three in the Occupy Movement 佔中三子. And 2019-2020 anti-extradition bill protests were jointly initiated by the Civil Human Rights Front 民間人權陣線, a Democrats' alliance in Hong Kong. Joshua Wong was not a leader in the alliance.

Fifth, while Joshua Wong often says in front of foreigners that he represents Hong Kong people, it is also often to see Hong Kong people putting on Facebook posts saying Joshua Wong does not represent them.

Last, of course, Joshua Wong, together with the whole self-proclaimed Democrats had only got 50% or arguably 60% supports in Hong Kong. At the same time, another 40-50% of Hong Kong locals are against them.

Foreigners generally believe Joshua Wong is the Hong Kong protest leader (as declared on the Wiki website) largely because he has been claiming himself as the representative for the Hong Kong people in front of foreigners. According to himself and his former democratic party Demosistō, one of their major tactics was to reach out to foreigners to gain their supports for their 'democratic movements'. They called it 'international frontline 國際戰線'. We will talk more about this topic in later parts of this book.

(At a glance, it sounds like to gain foreign support on his … independence movement for Hong Kong. A district's internal affairs would not require foreign supports, but a country's independence does require a lot of international support.

https://std.stheadline.com/politics/article/1298141/%E6%94%B F%E6%B2%BB-%E6%96%B0%E8%81%9E-%E7%BE%8E%E5%9C%8B-BLM-%E9%81%8B%E5%8B%95%E9%9C%87%E6%95%A3%E7%9 C%BE%E5%BF%97-%E5%9C%8B%E9%9A%9B%E6%88%B0%E7%B7%9A-%E8%A2%AB%E7%8B%A0%E6%89%B9%E9%BB%83%E4 %B9%8B%E9%8B%92%E9%81%93%E6%AD%89

To be fair, Joshua Wong is indeed a leader of Hong Kong people from one perspective.

To start with, on the day before he attended a court trial (September 29, 2020), he was spotted checking in to a top 5-star hotel with a sexy lady, who was reported to be a former best friend of his ex-girlfriend, together with his dog. But this was not the point. It was not a usual hotel room in a 5-star hotel, and not only an executive room, but a very expensive hotel room allowing animals to stay. The room charge was reported to be about HKD 6,000 per night (USD 772.5).

How frequently do you (or have you ever) take a hotel room at USD 772.5 per night, especially in your own town? You need to be quite wealthy to want to do this.

What has Joshua Wong's occupation been? His selling point, a student. Later, a politician, but never a senator. He had never been elected by the people to work for the Hong Kong government. He is a politician who established and ran his 2 political parties. And his father, Roger Wong, is in the middle class. (Roger Wong used to live in South Horizons, predominately for the middle class, for more than 10 years before he seeks asylum in Australia). According to Wiki and other sources, Joshua Wong has not had other jobs than working on political movements. (He does have a few political movies and a few political books. But I can tell you writing books normally give you little profits, if not losses.)

In other words, Joshua Wong's only income is donations from the public. Running political parties established by himself is, financially, the same as jobless. It is the same as running a not-for-profit company and there is not supposed to have any income other than donations. And starting up political organizations needs money, and his salary can only come from donations.

Living on donations from the public, 5-star top hotel rooms 五星級酒店, yacht cruise parties 遊艇派對 are parts of his usual life. And he lives in a serviced apartment 服務式住宅 in the expensive Hong Kong housing market. Therefore, he has long been criticized as having unexplained or untrackable incomes 支出與收入不相稱. Furthermore, incomes from donations are not taxable. With no VAT, GST and sales tax in Hong Kong, Joshua Wong is a full-time politician who is not quite a taxpayer.

https://m.orangenews.hk/details?recommendId=139029

https://eastweek.my-magazine.me/main/99171

Not only so, the money of the 2 political parties he ran, Solarism 學民思潮 and Demosistō 香港眾志, was found to have gone astray. Since the incorporation of Solarism in 2011 to 2015, the bank account for public donations has been more than HKD 2,500,000 (USD 234,000). However, when Solarism was disbanded, only HKD 1,400,000 was in the bank account, in which more than HKD 400,000 (USD 52,000) disappeared and Joshua Wong had been unable to explain how.

After that, his new political party, Demosistō, had received more than HKD 21,600,000 donations (USD 2,805,000) between 2016 to 2020, which Joshua Wong had never been able to tell the public where the money had gone.

黃之鋒先後創立的「學民思潮」、「香港眾志」都涉出現帳目混亂的情況；其中前者自 2011 年成立後，以社團戶口接受市民捐款，至2015年儲備一度超過250萬元；而至2016年該組織解散時，戶口只餘 145 萬元；而當中有 40 多萬元的去向是沒有向公眾交代過。後者在 4 年間更籌得超過 2160

萬元，但當該組織停止會務後，至今仍沒有人交代組織的資金去向。

With no official income, he was donated by the public so impressively and did not even need to explain how he spent the money he received and barely needed to pay tax. Wasn't he a king? Wasn't he a leader of the society?

Comparing with the Chief Executive in Hong Kong, Carrie Lam, her yearly salary in 2020-21 is HKD 5,210,000 (521 萬元) (USD 670,500). That means Joshua Wong's democratic parties received 4 times Hong Kong Chief Executive's yearly salary!!

https://wealth.hket.com/article/2609578/%E3%80%90%E7%89%B9%E9%A6%96%E4%BA%BA%E5%B7%A5%E3%80%91%E6%9E%97%E9%84%AD%E6%9C%88%E5%A8%A5%E5%B9%B4%E8%96%AA%E5%8A%A0%E8%87%B3521%E8%90%AC%20%20%E5%90%84%E5%9C%B0%E9%A0%98%E5%B0%8E%E4%BA%BA%E8%96%AA%E9%87%91%E9%82%8A%E5%80%8B%E6%9C%80%E9%AB%98%EF%BC%9F

Also, from the above, his donation incomes increase vastly when the relationship between Hong Kong people and their government and police worsen significantly from 2015 to 2020. When the people hate their government, Joshua Wong has a value to the people to 'speak out (the problems)' and confront the government for them. It is very different from 1989 Beijing students, who had not established any political parties and had not asked anyone for donations.

Joshua Wong had denied accusations on pro-China newspapers, Wen Wai Po 文匯報 and Tai Kung Po 大公報, that he had taken a great deal of money for personal use from the donations to his political parties. Joshua Wong clarified that he had never bought a property. He said he had never received a cent from Demosistō's donation '自己從來沒有收取任何眾志款項'.

However, none of my above quotes about his donation amounts and donations going astray was from the two pro-China newspapers that he had denied claims on. Instead, my above quotes were from mainstream Hong Kong newspapers such as East Weekly (similar reports on the same topic on other newspapers were not quoted here).

Furthermore, if he truly 'had never received a cent from Demosistō's donation' as he claimed, then it is worse – usually, even for charitable organizations, directors and shareholders do gain salary or remuneration from the full-time work. If not, what did he live on? Running the political party Demosistō was his full-time occupation. His father was only in the middle class and could not possibly and would not possibly let his son get no jobs and have no income. How did he pay the 5-star top hotel room bills with the girl and the dog we saw in the above post? Obviously, he lies.

See Joshua Wong's post to deny claims from the 2 pro-China newspapers:

https://www.facebook.com/photo?fbid=3147152465377240&set=a.313299448762570

But it was not the only time Joshua Wong lied. Remember the first political party he established, 'Scholarism' 學民思潮? He calls himself a 'scholar' in front of English-speaking foreigners. And in front of Hong Kong people, he calls himself '學民' (student / a learning civilian). Everyone in Hong Kong knows that he is no scholar at all (refer to my book 1, *Hong Kong Protest Leaders - Sick Facts that Western countries do not know*). If he called his political party 'Scholar' 學者 in the Hong Kong language, everyone would laugh at him. But he intentionally deceived English-speaking foreigners by wrongly translating his political party's name as 'Scholarism' which did not match the name in the Hong Kong language and he definitely was not a scholar.

Let us look at his other lies.

In July 2020, Joshua Wong **denied the 3 charges** of incitement 煽惑、organisation and involvement in illegal assembly 組織及參與未經批准集結 in the siege of police headquarters on June 22, 2019.

However, he later **pleaded guilty to the same charges** in November 2020 after discussion with lawyers. But there might be another reason: In December 2020, Joshua Wong said that the police had captured his iPhone XR on his arrest. According to Joshua's Facebook post, he later received a message from the police that his Whatsapp and Telegram message was read by the police and would be used as evidence for his charges of incitement.

In his Whatsapp and Telegram messages, Joshua Wong was discussing his plan on how to build up conflicts between protesters and the police in what he called a 'peaceful protest' when he asked his supporters to attend it.

His Whatsapp and Telegram messages were the reason why he changed to plead guilty. Most of the foreign press emphasized he was jailed for 'unauthorised assembly' in this siege of the police headquarters, downplaying his plans to build up conflicts as his Whatsapp and Telegram messages had revealed. His planned incitement was the biggest reason for his imprisonment.

The Guardian has said that Joshua Wong was jailed for pro-democracy protests, saying they were 'inciting others to attend' instead of the truth that his 'intentionally inciting conflicts with the police':

https://www.theguardian.com/world/2020/dec/02/hong-kong-activist-joshua-wong-jailed-over-protest-police-hq

Joshua Wong then accused the police of violating his human rights for hacking his phone, reading his Whatsapp and Telegram messages without his consent. However, he did not deny the contents of his Whatsapp and Telegram messages.

https://today.line.me/hk/v2/article/Jm15Z7

Does Joshua Wong have a general knowledge of international standards? In fact, both the United States and Australian government authorities have been wishing Whatsapp to provide access to messages for investigation and spotting criminal and terrorists' activities. As I had mentioned in my book, *I'm a Romance Scam IT Detective*, Whatsapp messages are encrypted and are frequently used by criminals.

https://www.securitymagazine.com/articles/91402-facebook-refuses-to-give-law-enforcement-access-to-its-messaging-app-whatsapp https://www.news.com.au/technology/online/security/australias-proposed-new-cyber-legislation-to-give-police-greater-access-to-content-on-smartphones/news-story/36683241a8799aaadf9b2dcbf3f938fa

Please note that in the above 2 quotes, Australian and the United States governments were requesting access to end-to-end encryption which is even deeper and broader than Joshua Wong's case where his iPhone was captured on his arrest. Hong Kong police got his Whatsapp messages from his end on the physical phone and did not need to hack into the end-to-end encryption on the Internet. Joshua Wong's case sounds like a usual criminal investigation procedure.

It is how Joshua Wong always looks for whatever excuses to accuse the police without looking into International standards. He wants to distract the public from actual evidence of his crimes.

In fact, his Whatsapp and Telegram messages were not that surprising. As illustrated above, Joshua Wong can only get donations, and more and more donations, when the Hong Kong locals are angry about the government and the police.

Some Chinese defamed Joshua Wong and Agnes Chow as Vietnamese descendants (not Chinese race as the vast majority of Hong Kong people are. Refer to Chapter Q1), explaining why he goes against China.

Joshua Wong has denied it, saying he has at least 4 generations in China with no relationship with Vietnam ... Hang on, so what is Joshua Wong's race? Hong Kong has been a part of China for a thousand years before Hong Kong becomes a British Colony from 1842 to 1997, except in World War II which Hong Kong was reigned by the Japanese for 3 years and 8 months. Also, the vast majority of Hong Kong people today are descendants of Chinese immigrants, if not themselves are Chinese immigrants. Joshua Wong's denial that he is Vietnamese implies he is Chinese.

So, why does Joshua Wong say he is not Chinese? Maybe he is Chinese who does not know himself is Chinese? Or he knows he is Chinese but he lies?

* 禍港四人幫 (the Gang of four who destroys Hong Kong) refers to 1) Jimmy Lai, the founder and owner of Apple Daily. 2) Martin Lee Chu-ming, who has been a senator in the Legislative Council both before and after Hong Kong returns to China. He was previously one of the barristers who drafted the Hong Kong Basic Law used under one country, two systems. 3) Anson Chan Fang On-sang, a retiree who used to be the Chief Secretary of Hong Kong, which was the second-highest position in the British colony. It was the highest position a Hong Kong local could take because the highest position, the governor, must be a British. Refer to Chapter L6, the pensioner had somehow received donations from Jimmy Lai after her retirement, despite she has been receiving a handsome pension from the Hong Kong government even after it returned to China. 4) Albert Ho Chun-yan, who used to be a candidate for the Chief Executive. He was the former chairman of the Hong Kong Alliance in Support of Patriotic Democratic Movements of China.

Read this pro-China newspaper to learn what the Chinese government says about the Gang of four who destroys Hong Kong':

http://www.takungpao.com.hk/news/232109/2019/0819/337946.html

**佔中三子 (the Three in the Occupy Movement) refers to Benny Tai, Chan Kin-man and Reverend Chu You-ming. Occupy Central in 2014 was their idea.

L4. Agnes Chow the actress

As mentioned in the previous chapter, some Chinese defamed Agnes Chow Ting and Joshua Wong as Vietnamese descendants (not Chinese descendants that the vast majority of Hong Kong people are. Refer to Chapter Q1). Joshua Wong had denied it. But Agnes Chow had never denied it. Does that mean Agnes Chow is indeed Vietnamese? Or, more likely, Agnes Chow simply does not even know her ancestors and her race ...

A politician who does not know where she is from and who herself is ...

Let us go back to the topic of the actress. Watch the below video (0:45-0:52). Agnes Chow put her hands behind with a cloth covering them. Looks like she had been handcuffed? Many newspapers did report that Agnes Chow was handcuffed (rudely treated by the police) when she was arrested. This made her gain sympathy from foreigners, especially the Japanese.

Watch more (1:01): A hand tidied up Agnes Chow's hair after she got into the prison car. She had forgotten that she was (pretending to be) handcuffed.

Since then, many anti-protest Hong Kong locals call her an actress.

https://www.youtube.com/watch?v=VJ2zrYDjTD8

But it was not the only time. When Agnes Chow was sentenced to 10 months' imprisonment, she cried. Apple daily reported that she cried pathetically. However, Agnes Chow soon clarified in her Facebook post that she was actually dropping tears of joy 喜極而泣 for being sentenced to jail.

Why did she insist she was dropping tears of joy 喜極而泣 for being sentenced to jail, not tears of fear or regretfulness? Analysis suggested that it was because they had been praising unlawful righteousness and they want this to continue in Hong Kong society. They have been encouraging people in society, especially youngsters, to break the laws and orders to fight for righteousness (democracy, in their theory). Some extremists suggest it is a glory to get criminal records or be jailed. (Refer to Jimmy Lai's interview with the foreign press just before he was sentenced and the last page of this book.)

Since then, many anti-protest Hong Kong people have been laughing at Agnes Chow for enjoying her tears of joy in prison. Although she has not been a good actress, her dramas can be quite entertaining.

Don't worry about her. Her politician friend had revealed that she wanted to join cookery classes in prison to learn to make cakes 蛋糕班.

https://hkgpao.com/articles/1018198

However, her dramas could not last long. When she was released from prison in Jun-2020, she said that she needed to take a break (from the democratic movements) and look after her body. Now, she no longer insists on fighting for democracy at all costs, at least not herself. On her release, there were only a few supporters in the scene screaming to support her. Her parents, whom she previously said were her biggest supports, were not there by her side on her release.

According to Apple Daily, there were 幾十人 (30-90 people) screaming to support Agnes Chow on her release. However, according to the actual videos, there were only very few odd voices saying, 'Add oil!' Others are just journalists or perhaps passers-by.

https://news.mingpao.com/ins/%E6%B8%AF%E8%81%9E/article/20210612/s00001/1623457538836/%E5%91%A8%E5%BA%AD%E5%87%BA%E7%8D%84%E3%80%90%E7%9F%AD%E7%89%87%E3%80%91 (From 37:38)

Right after Agnes Chow was released from prison, she removed the majority of the contents in her Facebook account, leaving only a photo in 2020 and her birthday in 1996. Possibly it was to avoid responsibility and more imprisonment for what she had said/posted since the national security law was in effect in mid-2020. Her post of 'dropping tears of joy' was also removed.

https://hkgpao.com/articles/1022382

As of the time of writing, Agnes Chow is still under investigation on an alleged case of seeking foreign interference in Hong Kong's internal affairs under the new national security law. Let us kindly wish her another chance soon to drop her tears of joy again.

L5. Joshua Wong's Father: expected to be convicted, but imprisonments are political persecutions

Joshua Wong's father is Roger Wong Wai-ming. Multiple reports reveal that Roger Wong, his wife and his other children had entered Australia in late 2020. Due to insufficient hotel quarantine spots in Australia, Roger Wong and his family entered Australia when about 30000 Australian citizens were stranded overseas unable to return home.

At that time, only Australian citizens were allowed to enter Australia due to COVID-19 restriction, with very few exception cases including urgent needs for humanitarian reasons. Obviously, Roger Wong and his family use humanitarian reasons to get entry to Australia, saying he has a very urgent need to leave Hong Kong or he would be unfairly and dangerously treated by the Hong Kong government.

Roger Wong refused to verify whether he has moved to Australia or not. But for certain was that Roger Wong had sold his home in Ap Lei Chau, Hong Kong, at 10% lower than the market price in November 2020. At least, multiple Australian newspapers are saying he has migrated to Australia.

https://www.sbs.com.au/chinese/mandarin/zh-hant/activist-joshua-wong-s-family-moved-to-australia-reported

https://www.huaglad.com/zh-tw/aunews/20210120/417487.html

https://cn.theaustralian.com.au/2021/01/20/48719/

Hong Kong Protest Leaders - Sick Facts that Western Countries do not know 2

As he used humanitarian reasons to enter Australia, what kind of danger did he face if he stayed in Hong Kong?

Looking at recent Chinese history, parents of arrested or killed students in the 1989 Tiananmen Massacre were able to attend TV interviews when they continue to live in China without hiding their identities.

Even the highest-profile student leaders in 1989 Tiananmen Square who have been wanted by China, Wang Dan 王丹 and Chai Ling 柴玲, have both met with their parents who continued to live in China. 吾爾開希 Örkesh Dölet's parents were not granted a visa to leave China but had never been arrested or tortured. 1989 Beijing student leader 吾爾開希 Örkesh Dölet, an asylum seeker in the United State, has since been fighting for the right to enter China. He is currently staying in Taiwan. None of their parents in China have been reported to be arrested by China or tortured by China.

The Chinese government may prosecute political criminals, but not their parents or family members.

https://www.bbc.com/zhongwen/trad/chinese_news/2011/09/110923_wangdanparents_byjames.amp

Roger Wong's humanitarian reasons to gain entry into Australia are purely imaginative.

So, why does Roger Wong need to leave Hong Kong and seek asylum in Australia? Perhaps he fears revenge by anti-protest civilians in Hong Kong – so many people get their children arrested for being involved in violent attacks in his son's declared 'peaceful protests'. (Refer to the last Chapter.)

Roger Wong, aged 57, was not qualified to enter Australia through skilled migration as it is limited to those at or under 45 years old. At his age, the only way for the married man to enter was by investment (which he did not appear to have sufficient funds) or seeking asylum with whatever excuse.

The entry of migrants like Roger Wong and his family into Australia will increase the social burden as they are unable to contribute much to the economy or society, except that he was good at lying and supporting unlawful righteousness. Refer to the coming session.

With about 30000 Australian citizens stranded overseas unable to get home, Roger Wong got a priority over them to enter Australia by saying democracy and faking the threat to be arrested in Hong Kong. Perhaps it is what he means by civil rights and human rights.

So, what is Roger Wong's view on the democracy movements? And what did he say about his son being jailed? Let us watch his interview:

The subject of his interview: Faulty is the father who does not teach his children the correct values - Roger Wong's ridiculous values 【養不教、父之過】黃之鋒爸爸三大歪理「離晒譜」

https://www.youtube.com/watch?v=uRZCfC5aWwo

(0:15) **Roger Wong** said, 'To be honest, we have expected that he (my son Joshua Wong) would be sentenced to the criminal penalty of community service order. But later, things suddenly got worse, saying he might be jailed. I was shocked! Wah! This society has gone so far ... 坦明講, 他判社會服務令的時候都是預計之內, 但之後突然急轉直下, 就說可能會坐監. 我覺得這個我是 shock 的, 我覺得社會原來是到了這個地步.'

(0:35) **Former chairperson of Hong Kong Lawyer Association (Bar Association), Paul SHIEH Wing-tai responded**, 'If you are unhappy about the court's decision, you can always appeal. As you (Joshua Wong) always say it is civil disobedience, you had declared you are fearless (of penalties). Then there is no bargaining on the punishment you will receive. No one has ever promised which sentence you must only receive. In human history, no one under civil disobedience has ever bargained on what penalty terms he/she should get. 法院判詞你不滿意, 你可以上訴. 你以公民抗命的角度來看, 抗命者一早話了無畏無懼. 無人應承你一定係某一種判決. 歷史上公民抗命, 也沒有人去斟酌刑期長短.'

(0:57) **Roger Wong** said, 'From his sentence, I can see very obvious political persecutions. Use your common sense: any sentence should be finalized once the jail term has been finished. Now they 'extract' (what have not been punished) from the same case, isn't it political persecutions? 今次判決, 我就見到好明顯的政治逼害. 用常理來想, 任何一個犯了案的人已經服了刑, 其實應該是了斷了. 服完了刑再抽出來, 還不是秋後算帳嗎? 我還可以怎樣形容?'

(1:20): **Senior Lawyer, Winnie Tam responded**, 'Lawyer for the defence originally had an intention to appeal. As a result, the first action must be completed before the Attorney can re-assess the jail term. Thus, from the timing point of view, they must first complete the community service order. This is pretty standard. All criminal offences in the court have this same procedure. You would have completed certain jail terms when you are waiting for an appeal, your total jail terms will be deducted with the corresponding time when an ultimate sentence is determined by the Court of Appeal. In Joshua Wong's case, as you can see, the Court of Appeal has deducted his jail terms. These are just a matter of procedure. There is no sign that the Attorney has any bad intention. 辯方那邊, 起初也有一個上訴的企圖, 令那個動作必須要完結, 律政師才能作刑期覆核. 所以令到時間上, 他們要履行社會服務令, 其實好均真的. 在一切刑事量刑都是這樣. 如果等上訴期間, 服了刑, 去到最終的判刑, 就會減回相應的刑期. 今次都看到上訴庭做了一個折扣的形式, 所以其實不是說, 從程序方面, 不能說這顯示出律政可有不好的企圖.'

(2:08) **Roger Wong** said, '(They) always say (the judge) has no political intention. It was clearly written in the verdict – the judge disagrees with the idea of unlawful righteousness. 成日話完全沒有政治動機, 其實爭論什麼呢? 法官在判詞中已經寫出來, 他自己的政治傾向. 他政治傾向是什麼? 就寫明違法達義, 其實他是完全不贊成.'

(2:25) **Chairperson of Hong Kong Lawyer Association (Bar Association). Paul Lam Ting-kwok responded**, 'Can't you read the whole verdict? When you don't, how can you gain a true understanding of what the legal justifications in the verdict are? The judge has to follow the law and the evidence, not whatever he wishes. 看文件當然要上文下理全部看完, 你才能真正了解到法律的理據在哪裡. 法官判案, 他自己不是任意妄為, 法官都是依從法律證據判案.'

From the above, does he have any basic legal knowledge? He just explains everything with political prosecutions and political intentions of the judges.

And Roger Wong's values are unlawful righteousness and civil disobedience.

L6. Jimmy Lai and Apple Daily, the pro-democracy newspaper

In recent years, Apple daily has been crowned as a pro-democracy newspaper. Its boss, Jimmy Lai, was given Gwen Ifill Press Freedom Award by Committee to Protect Journalists in 2021. He was also honoured with the Truman-Reagan Medal of Freedom by the Victims of Communism Memorial Foundation in 2021.

Hang on! Why would a newspaper be pro-democracy? Shouldn't newspapers be as neutral as possible? Why have all of the awards he received been about freedom? None about credibility, accuracy or the quality of writing? Anyway, Apple Daily was surely extraordinary, compared to other newspapers, at least, from the 'freedom' point of view.

Why was it named 'Apple' Daily? Did it mean this newspaper was healthy? Did it mean readers would need it every day? At a glance, it seemed to be what it meant. However, 'Apple' has another special character. 'Apple' is believed to be the forbidden fruit that Eve and Adam failed to resist. 'Apple' implies the temptation that humans fail to resist, bringing sin into the world. And it was exactly what Jimmy Lai meant when he named his newspaper.

Apple Daily was established in 1995, 2 years before Hong Kong returned to China. I was a high school student at that time. It was an exciting day. My parents, myself and everyone were all excited, somehow. Why? First, its price was a few times cheaper than a usual newspaper when it was first launched. Apple Daily beat other newspapers with a super cheap price. Soon, a few smaller newspapers bankrupted. Apple Daily then gradually increased their newspaper's price to the same price as the surviving ones.

Second, it was related to its marketing. When Apple Daily first launched, it was presented to be special. Indeed, ridiculous front pages, interesting fonts and a lot of comic-like news reporting on rape or sexually related topics. It looked like an entertainment magazine. Therefore, for the grassroots and less-educated civilians who did not like reading serious topics or serious newspapers, Apple Daily was really attractive and easy to read.

In high schools, students were encouraged to subscribe to newspapers. We had the options of South China Morning Post, Sing Tao Daily and Wen Wei Po. Apple Daily had never been on the menu. Why? As mentioned, it had been more like an entertainment newspaper with low credibility and poor writing skills. Students could not possibly enhance their literacy skills or learn something positive by reading Apple Daily.

If you have read my book 1, *Hong Kong Protest Leaders - Sick Facts that Western countries do not know*, you may remember that Apple Daily had confessed to paying someone money to get prostitutes for the sake of making up news on their cover page in 1998. It was only 3 years after it was first launched. I had also shown you statistics that the credibility of Apple Daily had always been as low as pro-China newspapers from 2001 to 2013.

Undoubtedly, Apple Daily was a newspaper with the most freedom – Jimmy Lai had not only confessed paying people to make up news, but Apple Daily had also pleaded guilty in multiple defamation cases in court.

https://newbloommag.net/2019/05/06/want-want-apple-suit/

https://www.scmp.com/news/hong-kong/politics/article/2169320/media-chief-sue-hong-kong-newspaper-apple-daily-over-altered

https://hongkongfp.com/2016/09/30/journalism-watchdog-shocked-as-cy-leung-accuses-apple-daily-of-defamation/

http://orientaldaily.on.cc/cnt/news/20101225/00176_021.html

Apple Daily had been convicted for defamation against different companies and people many times. Former Chief Executive CY Leung had said that Apple Daily had the most defamation conviction amongst newspapers. In 1998, Apple Daily said that a female lawyer absconded with dirty money without sufficient evidence. As a result, the female lawyer suffered from depression and miscarried. Apple Daily was convicted for defamation and needed to compensate more than HKD 3,200,000 (USD 411,800) to the lady.

In 2010, Next Magazine (also owned by Jimmy Lai) claimed that Chinese Shampoo BAWANG causes cancer. The claim had led to an enormous loss in sales of BAWANG. Next Magazine was convicted for defamation. The judge blames Next Magazine for rough research, superficiality and not up to professional standards. Next Magazine by Jimmy Lai was convicted for defamation and had compensated HKD 3 million (USD 386,000) to BAWANG:

https://www.scmp.com/news/hong-kong/law-crime/article/1951576/next-magazine-pay-bawang-shampoo-makers-hk3-million

In 2019, Apple Daily smeared Frederick Ma Si-hang, the former chairman of MTR Corporation, for allegedly having a conflict of interests for travelling on a private plane of Lui Che-woo, the managing director of K. Wah Group. Apple Daily by Jimmy Lai later apologised to the two gentlemen for misreporting. Frederick Ma condemned Apple Daily twice for substantially false reporting and terrible operations. Lui Chi-woo said that Apple Daily's report was pure defamation.

https://orientaldaily.on.cc/cnt/news/20190712/mobile/odn-20190712-0712_00176_033.html

It ended up Frederick Ma was not an employee and thus could not possibly have a conflict of interests. And the incident Apple Daily had reported happened years ago (not the last year Apple Daily had reported as), before Frederick Ma took the position in MTR Corporation. And even the private plane did not belong to Lui Che-woo. Everything Apple Daily had reported was wrong!

Defame many. If no one sues it, then it is good. If someone sues it, then apologise or pay compensation – it had been the usual Apple Daily way of news reporting.

That was Apple Daily's freedom of speech and press freedoms.

Nevertheless, Apple Daily's credibility had suddenly raised dramatically in the 2019 democratic movements. It was not because they had changed the management team, nor changed the journalists. They had only changed their target for defamation from individuals and companies to the Hong Kong government and the police force.

In many countries, take Australia as an example, government bodies are not eligible to sue anyone for defamation even with all the evidence.

https://www.artslaw.com.au/images/uploads/Defamation_law_(REPLACES_BOTH_PRE_AND_POST_2006_VERSIONS).pdf

Thus, there were zero risks for Apple Daily to defame the Hong Kong government and their police force. Even if there was sufficient evidence for such defamation, Apple Daily would not be liable to any compensations or exposed to any criminal charges, until the national security law was imposed in mid-2020.

When Apple Daily closed down, my mother and one of my best friends in Hong Kong with a master's degree said that they would not want to read any other newspapers than Apple Daily. I asked this best friend why he trusted Apple Daily so much when so many of its news reports were later found to be fake. He said, 'On the Chinese national day, all other newspapers congratulated China on their front pages. Only Apple Daily reported other things else. Only Apple Daily did not receive money from the Chinese government.' So, it is wrong for a newspaper to bless its country? So, this 'democratic movement' is not about making China more democratic, but about kicking China out of Hong Kong.

In the olden days, democratic movements were for the good of the people; Now, for Apple Daily, the anti-China views had given it very loyal readers who only trust this newspaper. In Hong Kong, being crowned as pro-democracy does give solid business benefits, at least apparently. You will know why I say 'apparently' soon.

Being unable to sue Apple Daily for defamation did not mean its news reporting was accurate. former Commissioner of Hong Kong Police, Chris Tan Ping-keung had quoted the writing of Apple Daily for making up fake stories (without explicitly mentioning 'Apple Daily'). For example, Apple Daily had falsely reported that an Oscar academy award winner for Best Actor in a Supporting role said he 'supported Hong Kong rioters'. If you know Apple Daily, it later apologised for the false report.

https://www.hk01.com/%E6%94%BF%E6%83%85/624024/%E9%84%A7%E7%82%B3%E5%BC%B7%E4%B8%8D%E9%BB%9E%E5%90%8D%E6%89%B9-%E8%98%8B%E6%9E%9C-%E5%A0%B1%E9%81%93-%E7%94%9F%E5%AE%89%E7%99%BD%E9%80%A0-%E8%8B%A5%E6%B6%89%E5%81%87%E6%96%B0%E8%81%9E%E5%9C%8B%E5%AE%89%E9%9C%80%E8%99%95%E7%90%86

Since the anti-extradition bill protests in 2019, Apple Daily and Radio Television Hong Kong (RTHK) had been smearing the Hong Kong Police force. The Hong Kong police force has issued 127 letters of complaint to Apple Daily in only 17 months, meaning 1 letter of complaint every 4 days. The Hong Kong Police Force had bought their complaints to the Communications Authority, which had issued multiple warnings to RTHK.

In the first 2 months of 2021, the Hong Kong Police Force had issued Apple Daily 2 letters of complaints about their smearing the use of the police welfare funds. Apple Daily had also used 'Indiscriminate arrest' as their news headlines to smear the police, saying 'a policeman may not only shoot (a protester) once but 4 or 5 times'. The police had clarified the side of the true story in many press conferences and social media.

According to Apple Daily, some were murdered by the police in the Prince Edward station and men and women were gang-raped by the police in San Uk Ling (Holding Center). It took months or a year for investigation departments to find out the truth and show evidence to the public. But the horror, sense of insecurity and escalated conflicts had already built up in the society in the months or a year. With more and more fake news taking time to get evidence to clarify, the people in the society have accumulated a large number of doubts towards the government and the police.

But we are still talking about the public who would read news reporting other than Apple Daily. Those who only trust Apple Daily would continue to live in the fake news and fake terror forever. Foreign press who had previously been pro-actively approached by Apple Daily will also continue to live in the fake news and no one will normally be too pro-actively to inform the foreign press and they will not drag these up. You will know what I refer to in later parts of this chapter.

https://orientaldaily.on.cc/cnt/news/20210303/mobile/odn-20210303-0303_00176_014.html

Many Hong Kong people call Apple Daily the 'Poisonous Apple' or the 'Poisonous Fruit' - well, it does match what Jimmy Lai said about 'Apple' as the forbidden fruit. There is a Facebook group for discussing Apple Daily's fake news reports:

https://www.facebook.com/groups/891852034719695/?ref=share

Now, Hong Kong people are divided into believing in 2 different sides of facts – the Apple Daily side of true stories, and the other newspapers side of true stories. If you believe in Apple Daily, then you continue to believe the lady with a ruptured eye and San Uk Ling gang rapes are all true stories.

So, other than the usual defamation, what other charges is Jimmy Lai facing? Here is an overview:

https://hk.on.cc/hk/bkn/cnt/news/20210604/bkn-20210604003517159-0604_00822_001.html

(Please click on pictures #2-3 to read the full Chinese version using a mobile phone. Some desktops cannot display the page properly.)

Date of alleged crimes	Charges	Status as of the time of writing
2017.06.04	**Criminal intimidation** against a journalist of another big local newspaper	The jury found him not guilty. But the Attorney has appealed to the high court.
2019.08.18	Organisation and involvement in an **illegal assembly**	Lai was found guilty and was sentenced to 12 months in prison. Lai has appealed against the conviction and the sentence.
2019.8.31	**Illegal assembly**	Lai has pleaded guilty. He was sentenced to 8 months in prison. Lai has appealed the sentence.
2019.10.1	Organisation and involvement in an **illegal assembly**	Lai has pleaded guilty. His jail terms accumulated to 20 months for the above 3 charges of multiple illegal assemblies.
2020.6.4	**Incitement, illegal assembly**	Lai has not yet decided whether he will plead guilty or not.
2016.6.27 to 2020.5.22	**Fraud**	A hearing was scheduled.
2020.7.1 to 2021.2.15	**National Security Law** –	Lai was arrested on December 11, 2020, and was granted bail on December 23, 2020. However, the

	i) seeking foreign interference to damage China's safety ii) conspiracy of seeking foreign interference to damage China's safety iii) single or a series of actions for **obstruction of justice**	Attorney appealed against the decision to grant him bail. The appeal was successful and Lai was re-arrested in February 2021. The hearing started in April 2021, and more hearings are scheduled.

In Lai's above charge on criminal intimidation in 2017 against a journalist of the Oriental Press Group, short videos were presented before the court. Lai had said to the journalist, 'I have taken your photo! I must get someone to '搞' the fucking you! 我實搵人搞 X 你!' Lai was found not guilty because the meaning of the word 搞 was considered literately ambiguous. However, in terms of usage, the sentence 搵人搞你 means to hire someone to kill, kidnap, rape, destroy or torture you or your family. We will see how it will go in the coming appeal.

The fraud charges from 2016 to 2020 was an interesting one. Jimmy Lai had hidden the fact that his another company, Dico Consultants Limited 力高顧問公司, has been secreting operating in the Apple Daily building that he had rented from Hong Kong Science and Technology Parks Corporation. The tenancy contract Lai has signed with the landlord has specified natures of business allowed to operate in the building. The operation of Dico Consultants Limited in the Apple Daily Building was an intentional violation of the tenancy contract, which had led to financial losses of the landlord and financial benefits of Apple Daily and Dico Consultants Limited, according to the accusation.

But it was not the most interesting part of this charge.

https://hd.stheadline.com/news/realtime/hk/2066016/%E5%8
D%B3%E6%99%82-%E6%B8%AF%E8%81%9E-
%E9%BB%8E%E6%99%BA%E8%8B%B1%E6%B6%89%E4
%B8%B2%E8%AC%80%E6%AC%BA%E8%A9%90%E6%A1
%88%E6%8A%BC%E6%98%8E%E5%B9%B43%E6%9C%88
%E9%96%8B%E5%AF%A9-
%E6%8E%A7%E6%96%B9%E7%94%B3%E8%AB%8B%E4%
BA%A4%E5%9C%8B%E5%AE%89%E6%B3%95%E5%AE%
98%E8%99%95%E7%90%86

The most interesting part of this matter was that **Dico Consultants Limited that Jimmy Lai owns has been donating huge amounts of money to multiple Hong Kong pro-democracy political parties, pro-democracy politicians and foreign government organizations and officers including the U.S. Deputy Secretary of Defense**, Paul Wolfowitz. In 2006-2014 alone, Dico Consultants Limited owned by Jimmy Lai had donated HKD 76,000,000 (USD 1,000,000).

Let us have a detailed look at the highest-profile parties that Jimmy Lai has been donating money to under the name Dico Consultants Limited. (Thanks to former Chief Executive CY Leung for the analysis and data collection from 2014 disclosure records of Jimmy Lai's public company Next Digital Limited 壹傳媒股民):

https://eastweek.my-magazine.me/main/100610

Recipient(s) of donation	Donation Amounts
June special event by Hong Kong Democratic Party, Civic Party and other 2 organizations	HKD 12,750,000 (USD 1,641,000)
Joseph Zen, a priest actively involved in Hong Kong pro-democracy movements	HKD 9,000,000 (USD 1,158,300)
Hong Kong Democratic Party	At least

	HKD 8,000,000 (USD 1,029,600)
Myanmar (Burma) Projects, reportedly anti-government bodies in Myanmar	HKD 5,320,000 (USD 684,800)
Hong Kong Civic Party	At least HKD 5,010,000 (USD 644,800)
Anson Chan, a high profile politician who was labelled by the Chinese government as a member of the 'Gang of four who destroys Hong Kong 禍港四人幫'	At least HKD 3,500,000 (USD 450,000)
Paul Wolfowitz, U.S. Deputy Secretary of Defense	HKD 780,000 (USD 100,000)
Pro-democracy politician, Long Hair	HKD 500,000 (USD 64,400)
Pro-democracy politician, Claudia Mo, who was found to have given multiple consultations to Benny Tai on the proposal of '10 steps to die/lose together 攬炒十步'	HKD 500,000 (USD 64,400)
Chu Yiu-ming, one of the Three 佔中三子 who proposed the Umbrella Movement (the Occupy Movement) in 2014	HKD 400,000 (USD 51,500)
Hong Kong Democracy development Network	HKD 400,000 (USD 51,500)
Democracy Special development projects	HKD 400,000 (USD 51,500)
Anonymous	HKD 1,690,000 (USD 217,500)

So, Jimmy Lai has been heavily funding the Hong Kong democratic movements and then made headlines on Apple Daily. Does it look similar to what he did in 1998 that he paid a man to get prostitutes and made headlines on Apple Daily? (Refer to my book 1, *Hong Kong Protest Leaders - Sick Facts that Western countries do not know*. It was not an allegation. Jimmy Lai had confused it.)

The judge of Jimmy Lai's fraud case had received a bomb threat and a death threat soon after denying him bail. To my memory, it was not only one judge in only one of his cases who had received death threats. Judges in more than his few cases have received death threats. Of course, the death threats might not come from his people. It might come from his supporters.

https://www.scmp.com/news/hong-kong/law-and-crime/article/3112720/hong-kong-magistrate-handling-jimmy-lais-fraud-case

https://www.thestandard.com.hk/breaking-news/section/4/160449/DoJ-condemns-death-threats-against-national-security-judge

These news reports were only in Hong Kong newspapers. Foreign newspapers only focus on his sentences or his being refused on bail, and do not tend to mention his judges were receiving death threats: https://www.nytimes.com/2021/05/28/world/asia/hong-kong-arrests-court.html

https://www.bbc.com/news/world-asia-china-55168823

The right-hand man of Jimmy Lai, Mark Simon, is a former CIA employee. He had also worked for the US Naval Intelligence Agency. Why would a normal newspaper hire a former foreign intelligence agency member for such an important position? Many have accused Jimmy Lai of colluding with the US government to ruin Hong Kong to initiate anti-China noises across the globe.

Media reports also revealed that Jimmy Lai had a lot of interactions with US senior officials in the periods of Hong Kong protests.

https://www.globaltimes.cn/content/1207151.shtml

https://www.scmp.com/news/hong-kong/article/1570781/im-not-spy-says-jimmy-lais-right-hand-man-mark-simon

On June 17, 2021, 5 company directors of Apple Daily were arrested under the new national security law for conspiring to collude with foreign countries or external forces to endanger national security.

According to a Senior Superintendent of the National Security Department of the Hong Kong Police Force, Steve Li Kawi-wah, Apple Daily had published a series of articles urging foreign authorities to impose sanctions against the Hong Kong government or the Chinese government since 2019 on printed newspapers and the Internet. However, the national security law was only in effect from June 30, 2020, thus, only his actions after that could violate the law.

Steve Li emphasized that the police value the importance of press freedom. He said, 'Unfortunately, this time the organization violating the national security law happened to be a newspaper. 今次要在傳媒機構執法是無可選擇，因為它（涉嫌）違反《港區國安法》。'

https://theinitium.com/article/20210617-evening-brief/

Being a newspaper does not mean one should be exempted from obeying the laws. Former Chief Executive CY Leung said, 'Requesting foreigners to impose sanctions against your own country is definitely a crime of treason, no matter which country you belong to.'

Jimmy Lai was reported to be related to the 'Hong Kong twelve 十二瞞逃' too. The 'Hong Kong twelve 十二瞞逃' were the 12 men arrested by Chinese customs for mistakenly entering the Chinese sea when they attempted to escape to Taiwan. (The actual translation should have been '十二 the twelve 瞞 secretly 逃 escaped')

One of the 12 men, Andy Li Yu-hin, 31, was originally charged with seeking foreign interference to damage China's safety, conspiracy assistance to criminals and illegally possess explosives. After he returned to Hong Kong, he pleaded guilty to seeking foreign interference to damage China's safety under the new national security law. He and Chan Tsz-wah, a paralegal aged 29, have become state witnesses against Jimmy Lai and Mark Simon for initiating and funding their activities to request foreign governments to impose sanctions against Chinese and Hong Kong governments and their officers from July 2020 to February 2021 (i.e., the period since the national security law was imposed until Jimmy Lai was jailed).

In the hearing, the lawyer said that Andy Li was responsible for financial (management) and approaching governments internationally. * Finn Lau 劉祖迪 (currently in exile) was responsible for marketing on social media. Principal organizers and fundings were by Jimmy Law and the ex-US intelligence agency, Mark Simon.

In June 2019, Chan Tsz-wah had met Mark Simon, who introduced him to Jimmy Lai. Soon, they suggested including Andy Li and Finn Lau in their operations. In January 2020, while in Taiwan, Jimmy Lai explained to them about his 4 steps to the subversion of the Chinese Communist government.

The group of people had proactively run 3 international marketing, condemning the Chinese Communist government, Hong Kong government and the Hong Kong Police Force on foreign newspapers of many countries. In one of the marketing events alone, Jimmy Lai first paid HKD 1,500,000 (USD 193,000) for Andy Li to advertise in foreign newspapers and expected later reimbursement from public donations organized by Andy Li. This group of people also invited foreign politicians to come to Hong Kong to monitor Hong Kong's elections. After that, Andy Li had sent a name list of Hong Kong and Chinese officials to the United States and request to impose sanctions against them.

After the Hong Kong national security law has become in effect, this group of people continued to urge the United Kingdom, Ireland and other 30 countries (totally 32 countries) to terminate their extradition bills with Hong Kong. (Australia, as an example, has immediately terminated its extradition bill with Hong Kong just after China announced the national security law in Hong Kong.)

After the arrest of Andy Li, Mark Simon had told Chan Tsz-wah that there would be no impact on their operations: Finn Lau would continue with his works in the United States to convince the US government to impose sanctions against China and Hong Kong. Mark Simon had also reminded Chan Tsz-wah that he may be arrested under the new national security law but guaranteed him that Jimmy Lai would assist him in fleeing to the United States. Mark Simon had told Chan Tsz-wah to, therefore, continue his tasks.

Andy Li and Chan Tsz-wah **agreed to the above details** and apologised to the people in the hearing. They pleaded guilty and are waiting for the sentence.

When Andy Li was arrested, Jimmy Lai and a few others were said to have helped Andy Li in his attempt to escape to Taiwan.

https://www.bloomberg.com/news/articles/2021-08-19/hong-kong-sees-first-guilty-pleas-under-national-security-law

Hong Kong Protest Leaders - Sick Facts that Western Countries do not know 2

https://news.tvb.com/local/611e32bc34b0316d729bc2d9/%E6%
9D%8E%E5%AE%87%E8%BB%92%E9%99%B3%E6%A2%9
3%E8%8F%AF%E6%89%BF%E8%AA%8D%E4%B8%B2%E
8%AC%80%E5%8B%BE%E7%B5%90%E5%A4%96%E5%9C
%8B%E5%8B%A2%E5%8A%9B%E5%8D%B1%E5%AE%B3
%E5%9C%8B%E5%AE%89%E7%BD%AA-
%E6%98%8E%E5%B9%B4%E4%B8%80%E6%9C%88%E5%8
6%8D%E6%8F%90%E8%A8%8A

According to the majority of foreign press, the closing down of Apple Daily was a result of China's cracking down on press freedom in Hong Kong. They also reported as if Apple Daily was profitable and largely loved by Hong Kong people, only forced to close down due to frozen funds of the company under the new national security law.

However, even Jimmy Lai disagreed with it. It was what Jimmy Lai said in his video:

'Dear everyone, I need your help. As the majority of companies had stopped their advertisements and the number of subscribers of Apple Daily had reduced from 800,000 to less than 600,000. It is now very difficult to run Apple Daily. Please support us and subscribe to Apple Daily. 我哋有事請大家幫忙 ... 因為廣告封殺及疫情爆發，報紙幾乎完全沒有廣告，訂閱人數亦由 80 萬下跌到不足 60 萬，令《蘋果日報》經營非常困難，呼籲市民支持訂閱。

The subject of Jimmy Lai's video was 'Apple Daily in danger. Difficult to operate. Himself (Jimmy Lai) has already lost HKD 550,000,000 (USD 70,785,071) 《蘋果》告急：經營困難，自己已墊支 5.5 億'. (Please note that this is a pro-protest website):

https://www.thestandnews.com/society/%E9%BB%8E%E6%99%BA%E8%8B%B1%E6%8B%8D%E7%89%87%E7%82%BA-%E8%98%8B%E6%9E%9C-%E5%91%8A%E6%80%A5-%E7%B6%93%E7%87%9F%E5%9B%B0%E9%9B%A3-%E8%87%AA%E5%B7%B1%E5%B7%B2%E5%A2%8A%E6%94%AF-5-5-%E5%84%84-%E5%91%BC%E7%B1%B2%E5%B8%82%E6%B0%91%E8%A8%82%E9%96%B1

When Apple Daily was first established in the 1990s, it was indeed profitable. In its best time, it used to sell 500,000 copies in a day. However, in the 2010s, the sale kept dropping from 260,000 copies per day in 2011 to 88,000 copies per day in 2020. See the statistics:

https://www.hk01.com/%E8%B2%A1%E7%B6%93%E5%BF%AB%E8%A8%8A/641049/%E8%98%8B%E6%9E%9C%E6%97%A5%E5%A0%B1-%E5%81%9C%E5%88%8A-%E5%A3%B9%E5%82%B3%E5%AA%92%E9%AB%98%E5%B3%B0%E6%9C%9F%E5%B9%B4%E6%94%B6%E5%85%A536%E5%84%84-2016%E5%B9%B4%E6%88%90%E6%A5%AD%E7%B8%BE%E5%88%86%E6%B0%B4%E5%B6%BA

Its anti-government reporting and false reports did bring it credibility by proving it was fearless. However, at the same time, many other people stopped touching Apple Daily due to the high volume of fake news and unneutral reporting.

On the last day of Apple Daily, most of the foreign press such as The Guardian reported that Hongkongers queued for hours to buy the final Apple Daily edition. However, it failed to mention other Hongkongers sipped champaign to celebrate the death of the poisonous fruit outside the Apple Daily building. They put Jimmy Lai's picture with label '人渣 Scum', holding banner 'Apple Daily finally paid for what it does. So excited for its closing down 蘋果日報終有報應, 執笠清盤大快人心 ' with celebration music.

https://hd.stheadline.com/news/realtime/hk/2108202/%E5%8D%B3%E6%99%82-%E6%B8%AF%E8%81%9E-%E8%98%8B%E6%9E%9C%E5%81%9C%E5%88%8A-%E6%9C%89%E5%B8%82%E6%B0%91%E5%88%B0-%E8%98%8B%E6%9E%9C-%E5%A4%A7%E6%A8%93%E5%A4%96-

%E9%96%8B%E9%A6%99%E6%AA%B3%E6%85%B6%E7%A5%9D

The final edition of Apple Daily sold very well. It is said that many individuals bought 10 or 20 copies of the final edition and gave them out as free gifts. This was why so many copies were sold.

* Finn Lau was the pioneer of the idea of 'Let us all die together'. He used username '我要攬炒 (I want to die/lose together)' to put on a post in the LIHKG discussion group (lihkg.com). Refer to my book 1, *Hong Kong Protest Leaders - Sick Facts that Western countries do not know*.

Benny Tai only further applied the idea in the election.

L7. Other pro-democracy newspapers in Hong Kong

Apple Daily was famous globally because Jimmy Lai the tycoon and his alliance had been proactively contacting foreign press and tell their side of 'true stories'. It was also because Apple Daily was one of the biggest newspapers in Hong Kong and its writings were frequently quoted or forwarded by the foreign press.

But Apple Daily was only a major press operated by or vastly fundings to the Hong Kong democratic movements, using the media to seek supports. The Stand News 立場新聞 and RTHK were other local ones.

Do you remember Denise Ho, who was with Joshua Wong presenting their case before a US congressional commission in September 2019? This Denise Ho was a company director of a local pro-democracy press, the Stand News.

https://hongkongfp.com/2019/09/17/live-hong-kong-activists-denise-ho-joshua-wong-testify-us-congressional-hearing-protests/

The Stand News 立場新聞 was established in the year of Umbrella Movement (Occupy movement) in 2014. 立場 does translate to 'Stand'. However, it does not mean 'Stand up' or 'Stand out'. Instead, it means 'the opinions we stand'. From the name alone, it really does not intend to be neutral.

Denise Ho, who has been presented as a Hong Kong pro-democracy activist, has been a famous pop singer in Hong Kong. You may remember I am a musician if you have listened to my previous audiobook about Internet scams and hackers. However, somehow, I have absolutely no memory of what songs Denise Ho had ever sung. She had been famous but not great enough to have her personal concert on the stage. At least, not a large personal concert.

Denise Ho and 5 others resigned from their positions as company directors of the Stand News a few days after Apple Daily closed down (i.e., almost 1 year after the new national security law was imposed). This Internet newspaper continues to operate after their resignation.

https://www.dimsumdaily.hk/stand-news-removes-all-opinion-pieces-published-in-may-2021-6-directors-including-denise-ho-resigned/

Denise Ho, a dual citizen of Canada and Hong Kong, had never been arrested under the new national security law. She was definitely in Hong Kong in 2020 and 2021. It was said that she has been running online personal concerts, asking for expensive subscription fees that only protesters would be willing to pay and support her.

(In early 2021, there had been rumours that Hong Kong no longer allows dual citizenships. It was a false report. I have been a dual citizen of Hong Kong and Australia and had not been told to give up either citizenship. What Chief Executive Carrie Lam said in early 2021 was that dual citizens are not allowed to seek foreign help to avoid being arrested if they commit crimes in Hong Kong, which had always been the case since Hong Kong returned to China. But many foreign journalists misinterpreted it as an end to dual citizenship.

Please note that dual citizenship is a privilege to Hong Kong people and not to Chinese nationals. Chinese nationals must give up their Chinese citizenship if they want to become Australian or Canadian citizens. Also, Hong Kong citizenship cannot co-exist with Chinese citizenship. Though rare, I did know someone who gave up her Hong Kong citizenship when she wanted to get Chinese citizenship for business convenience. Hong Kong is a part of China, but their citizenships are considered differently.)

The Radio Television Hong Kong (RTHK) was an interesting one – RTHK has been run with government's funding, but have long been criticised as spreading biased or fake news against the Hong Kong government and the Hong Kong police. (Refer to the previous chapter). The Director of Broadcasting, Leung Ka-wing, is an American citizen. Some accuse him of having an even closer link with the United States than Hong Kong but has been controlling a Hong Kong major channel.

After an enormous number of complaints, his position was replaced by Patrick Li.

https://en.wikipedia.org/wiki/RTHK#2021_management_change

RTHK used to have a lot of educational programs when I was in primary school. Unfortunately, these years, their political views have been very clear when news reporting is supposed to be as neutral as possible.

Not only newspapers but also some movies advocate going against the government or even attacks.

理大圍城 *Inside the Red Brick Wall* and 佔領立法會 *Taking back the Legislature* were documentary movies shown in the Hong Kong Arts Center in late 2020 **after the new national security law was in effect.**

Inside the Red Brick Wall was the recording of the conflicts or warzone between the police and the students in the Hong Kong Polytechnic University. If you have watched my Youtube videos, you would know students were creating weapons in the University.

Taking back the Legislature was the recording of protesters breaking into the Legislative Council and damaged the council on July 1, 2019. ('Take back' here actually means 'occupy'佔領 because the protesters had never owed the Legislative Council before the incident.)

https://zh.wikipedia.org/wiki/%E4%BD%94%E9%A0%98%E7%AB%8B%E6%B3%95%E6%9C%83_(%E7%B4%80%E9%8C%84%E7%89%87)

Let us watch how the 'peaceful' and 'unarmed' protesters broke into the Legislative Council. And the 'cold-blooded' policemen were only standing there, warning them not to break into the government building. The protesters ignored them and broken into the government building.

https://www.youtube.com/watch?v=ZUG853vHNig

And protesters damage the interior and things inside the government building after they broke into the Legislative Council:

https://www.youtube.com/watch?v=NNI5XjAR9x0

Some criticised these documentary movies as terrorism movies that heroized criminals. Even the most democratic countries would not allow such movies supporting terrorism to go in cinemas. Think about if the same happens to the United States or the United Kingdom - protesters 'take back' (actually occupy) the White House, or protesters 'take back' the Buckingham Palace. Can they make these heroic movies and publicly show them in the cinema?

Under the new national security law, these movies are showed legally in the Hong Kong Arts Center.

'Live as free people, but do not use your freedom as a cover-up for evil ...'

— 1 Peter 2:16

L8. Ted Hui, Hong Kong Asylum Seeker in Australia with few different criminal charges

On June 12, 2021, Ted Hui Chi-fung was interviewed by SBS news in a mini-Hong Kong pro-democracy protest in Sydney Town Hall, urging the Australian government to help them.

In this TV news interview, Ted Hui was reported to be a former Hong Kong Legislative Councillor. He was crowned as a human rights hero who fled Hong Kong under the threats of the new national security law. However, the most important parts of his stories were missing and he did not flee Hong Kong for the national security law. Read the details below.

Yes, Ted Hui was indeed a former Hong Kong Legislative Councillor elected by the people. However, when he escaped from Hong Kong in December 2020, he was on bail under 9 criminal charges when he worked for the Hong Kong government, facing 3 years jail terms. None of which were related to national security law at all. Here were how these happened:

https://zh.m.wikipedia.org/wiki/%E8%A8%B1%E6%99%BA%E5%B3%AF

https://www.hk01.com/%E6%94%BF%E6%83%85/557336/%E8%A8%B1%E6%99%BA%E5%B3%AF%E6%B5%81%E4%BA%A1-%E8%BA%AB%E8%B2%A09%E5%AE%97%E7%BD%AA%E4%B8%80%E8%A6%BD-%E5%85%B6%E4%B8%AD%E5%85%A9%E9%A0%85%E6%9C%80%E9%AB%98%E5%8F%AF%E7%9B%A3%E7%A6%813%E5%B9%B4

Scandals of Hong Kong Protest Leaders

Date/venue of the crimes	Charges	Details
2019.4.11 The Legislative Council of Hong Kong	1) Criminal dishonest use of computer 2) Common assault(s) 3) Obstructing government officer(s)	Ted Hui had robbed a mobile phone from a female government officer. He then rushed into a male toilet and read it for 10 minutes. CCTV was used as evidence of his crime.
2019.7.6 Tuen Mun Park Protest, Hong Kong	4) Criminally destroying properties 5) Obstruction of justice	Ted Hui had robbed a mobile phone from a civilian and destroyed it.
2020.5.8 The Legislative Council of Hong Kong	6) use of poison with an intention to harm a person 7) Contempt	Ted Hui poured stink water with decay plants 撥臭水 towards the chairperson in the Hong Kong Legislative Council, who was reviewing the new National Anthem Ordinance. Let us watch the video of Ted Hui throwing stink materials towards the chairperson in the Legislative Council: https://www.youtube.com/watch?v=vSjXdQO6YGQ
2020.6.4 The Legislative Council of Hong Kong	8) use of poison with an intention to harm a person 9) Contempt	Ted Hui, again, poured stink water with decay plants 撥臭水 towards the chairperson in the Hong Kong Legislative Council, who was reviewing the new National Anthem Ordinance.

87

It is Ted Hui's idea of democracy and human rights. When he was unhappy about what was discussed in the Legislative Council, or when there were not enough votes from other senators on what he wished, he just poured stink water toward other individuals in the Legislative Council - his workplace and a government building. And when he was unhappy with what civilians or other government officers did, he just stopped them by force. It is his idea of human rights and righteousness.

As a result of his crimes, especially the first one, Ted Hui was condemned by his democratic political party and had his **membership suspended**. His membership with the political party was later re-instated.

https://hk.on.cc/hk/bkn/cnt/news/20180425/bkn-20180425162243344-0425_00822_001.html

By saying the words 'democracy' and 'human rights' in a foreign country where people barely know him, suddenly Ted Hui's crimes have all been erased. He suddenly becomes a human rights fighter, not any more a human rights criminal when he goes to a foreign country where most people do not understand Hong Kong's languages (Cantonese / Traditional Chinese) and thus cannot read Hong Kong newspapers about him.

He was not charged under the new national security law when he fled Hong Kong. But he needed to ensure he became wanted under the new national security law, otherwise, he would not be qualified to gain asylum in a foreign country and will be sent back to Hong Kong and face the 3 years' jail terms for his other criminal offences.

To achieve this, he had to violate national security law after he fled. After going on exile, he said he changed to 'international battlefront' (or 'international frontline'), which means to seek international interference on Hong Kong's affairs or international supports for Hong Kong independence. This effectively made him violated the national security law.

And he has to say the bad of Hong Kong. He has to convince the world that Hong Kong legal system and human rights have been entirely corrupted. By doing so, he can avoid being checked on his criminal records in his place of citizenship and avoid being sent back to Hong Kong and be jailed when granted asylum in a foreign country.

Australian politicians, who do not understand Hong Kong languages, were so touched by his heroism. Labour Party in Australia even urged the current Prime Minister to give these Hong Kong asylum seekers **permanent residencies** instead of just temporary shelters.

There is another thing Ted Hui had probably not told the Australian government. According to Ted Hui's Facebook post when he announced his exile abroad, **he declared that he has an insistence on never migrating to a foreign country** as he loved Hong Kong very much. He said his exile abroad was to strengthen the international supports for democracy in Hong Kong. His speech was so touching and he soon asked his supporters in Hong Kong for long-term donations (Refer to Chapter L10). See the screenshot of his Facebook post here:

https://www.master-insight.com/%E8%A8%B1%E6%99%BA%E5%B3%AF%E5%AE%A3%E5%B8%83%E6%B5%81%E4%BA%A1-%E9%80%80%E5%87%BA%E6%B0%91%E4%B8%BB%E9%BB%A8-%E6%9C%AA%E6%B1%BA%E5%AE%9A%E5%9C%A8%E4%BD%95%E5%9C%B0%E5%81%9C%E7%95%99/

Well, we hope the Australian government would respect his decision and never grant him permanent residency as he told his supporters it would be his insistence. So, one day Ted Hui will have his visa ceased and get back to Hong Kong for the 3 years' imprisonment?

Since the announcement of the new national security law of Hong Kong in mid-2020, Australia had condemned China and had accepted a few criminals wanted by Hong Kong like Ted Hui. China surely dislikes it much, as Australia is denying the Chinese and Hong Kong governments' decisions on their internal affairs. It was the same as saying China/Hong Kong's legislative and law enforcement systems are completely rubbish.

Naturally, China was not happy.

Soon, China raised tariffs on Australian barley, red wines and other produce. China also told its people that Australia was a dangerous place for Chinese people and that they should not study or visit Australia. Obviously, China was imposing trade sanctions against Australia for interfering with its internal affairs. Surprisingly, Australian leaders did not notice these were trade sanctions and believed they could just resolve the trading tensions by giving them a call. To be honest, the Hong Kong opposition has been requesting foreign governments to impose sanctions against the Chinese government for not listening to them. Can't the Chinese government does the same and impose sanctions against a foreign government for interfering with their internal affairs and devaluing their legislative and law enforcement systems too?

Ted Hui, who originally fled to Denmark and then Britain, was believed to have been refused asylum in these 2 countries before heading to Australia. Same as Roger Wong, he was given priority to enter Australia in the time of COVID-19 when about 30000 Australian citizens were stranded overseas unable to get home due to insufficient hotel quarantine spots.

Australia, the third choice of Ted Hui, believes itself is helping Hong Kong's innocent people will continue to confront China and harm its own economy for the welfare of these criminals, sadly.

Ted Hui originally declared that he intended to settle in Britain, but probably got refused.

https://www.scmp.com/news/hong-kong/politics/article/3112370/former-hong-kong-opposition-lawmaker-ted-hui-breaks-silence

To look at the bright side, luckily, Ted Hui will probably not increase the financial burdens of Australia as he had started his fund-raising campaign to ask his Hong Kong supporters for donations. He can gain way more than you or me. (Refer to Chapter L10) However, it would not be able to compensate the trade loss due to accepting this wanted criminal. And attracting people like Ted Hui with multiple criminal charges of different kinds is really harmful to Australia's society.

And will taking up Ted Hui bring the culture of pouring stink water in senators' meetings into Australia?

Other than the above twice, in the below video, Ted Hui was pouring water towards the chairperson in a meeting in the government's Legislative Council. Apparently, he was not charged this time, probably because water is not as offensive as the stinking water he poured in the other 2 times.

https://www.youtube.com/watch?v=g1irZyXlb3s

How can one not be sorry for Australia for having absorbed such a criminal into its society?

And how would Australia not know Ted Hui is a criminal with multiple charges and gave him entry when so many Australians are waiting for a spot to get home in the first place? Because Australia simply do not know Hong Kong's situation and decided not to recognize Hong Kong's law anymore, thus did not check Ted Hui's criminal records there or did not recognize his criminal records there.

Hope that the Australian government can either open its eye to the actual problems Hong Kong is facing or just stop interfering with other country's internal affairs without looking into the details.

As a separate note, I had personally written to Australia SBS news, complaining about their biased report about Ted Hui for erasing all his other charges for his saying 'democracy'. SBS Ombudsman responded that by emphasizing his charges under national security law and intentionally missing out all his criminal charges for attacking other people is 'consistent with Code 2.2, the absence of additional detail about which and how many charges he would face did not make the report unbalanced, inaccurate or unfair.'

L9. Nathan Law, the right person at the right time

Amongst the 3 most famous 'Hong Kong student protest leaders', Nathan Law Kwun-chung was the smartest one. He always knows to get the most advantages out of the situation and quit at the right time when he knew there were no more he could gain.

Graduated from the 2nd worst university in Hong Kong, Lingnan University, Nathan Law became internationally reputable for his outstanding position in the Umbrella Movement (Occupy Movement) in 2014 and was therefore admitted to Yale University. He started his study at Yale University in Aug-2019 when he and his teams were urging Hong Kong students to go on university strikes for the 2019-20 protests.

But it was not the best of Nathan Law. When China announced the new national security law, his counterpart, Joshua Wong, who was still dreaming to become a Prime Minister of an independent Hong Kong and decided to continue his pro-independence movement. In contrast, Nathan Law knew he could no longer gain vast donations in Hong Kong without violating the new national security law. He had already become well equipped with a reputable university master degree in Yale and chose to get on the plane just a few days before the new national security law was in effect on June 30, 2020.

Please note that Hong Kong's new security law was not retroactive. You can see many other activists who seek foreign sanctions against Hong Kong only before the law was in effect were never arrested. Therefore, when **Nathan Law fled Hong Kong before the law was in effect, he was definitely cleared of any charges under** the new national security law – anything he had done before June 30, 2020, could not be considered under the new law.

https://news.rthk.hk/rthk/en/component/k2/1534945-20200630.htm

Nathan Law only became wanted under the new national security law after he sought asylum, defaming Hong Kong and Chinese governments in foreign countries in his exile. Yes, **he must ensure he became wanted by the Hong Kong government under the new national security law. Otherwise, he would not be qualified to gain asylum in a foreign country.** This probably explained why he only sought asylum in the United Kingdom 5 months after he arrived there. See the timeline here:

https://zh.wikipedia.org/wiki/%E7%BE%85%E5%86%A0%E8%81%B0#%E6%B5%81%E4%BA%A1%E8%8B%B1%E5%9C%8B

In 1989, wanted student leaders all needed to be smuggled out of mainland China before they can board their flights outside China to seek asylum in a Western country. But in the Hong Kong protests, people who claim they are under the threats of China's power such as Roger Wong, Nathan Law and many other unfamous ones can just go through Hong Kong customs and board their flights in Hong Kong airport to seek asylum in Australia, the United Kingdom, Germany and other countries.

And we must appreciate Nathan Law's art of speaking. He said, 'I will never, ever give up my Hong Kong citizenship!! … If I do nothing, I will have no identity (when my Hong Kong passport expires). After a lot of struggle in my heart, I decided to seek asylum in the United Kingdom. 永不放棄香港人身份 … 假若我再不行動，我就只能成為一個沒有護照、身份的人。經歷一連串思想掙扎後，我決定在英國申請政治庇護'

Nathan is really good at speaking. Both the United Kingdom and Hong Kong accept multi-citizenship. All who are obtaining multi-citizenship with these countries will never be asked to give up their original citizenship, and naturally, they would not because there is no need to and no advantage. Like Denise Ho in Chapter L7 and myself, we are dual citizens of both Hong Kong and another country and have never given up our Hong Kong citizenships because no one has ever requested us to. Nathan Law was only doing what everyone does but described that as if he did it for his loyalty to Hong Kong and its people, only to enhance his imagine and continue to gain donations for his 'international frontline' from his supporters for Hong Kong independence.

https://www.hk01.com/%E6%94%BF%E6%83%85/564670/%E5%90%91%E8%8B%B1%E6%94%BF%E5%BA%9C%E7%94%B3%E6%94%BF%E6%B2%BB%E5%BA%87%E8%AD%B7-%E7%BE%85%E5%86%A0%E8%81%B0-%E6%B0%B8%E4%B8%8D%E6%94%BE%E6%A3%84%E9%A6%99%E6%B8%AF%E4%BA%BA%E8%BA%AB%E4%BB%BD

Please note that it is a pro-protest website:

https://www.thestandnews.com/politics/%E6%B1%BA%E5%AE%9A%E5%9C%A8%E8%8B%B1%E7%94%B3%E8%AB%8B%E6%94%BF%E6%B2%BB%E5%BA%87%E8%AD%B7-%E7%BE%85%E5%86%A0%E8%81%B0-%E6%B0%B8%E4%B8%8D%E6%94%BE%E6%A3%84%E9%A6%99%E6%B8%AF%E4%BA%BA%E8%BA%AB%E4%B

B%BD-
%E6%B0%B8%E7%84%A1%E4%BC%91%E6%AD%A2%E5
%90%91%E6%94%BF%E6%AC%8A%E7%BA%8F%E9%AC
%A5

After he was granted a protection visa by the United Kingdom, he publicly urged his new country to grant asylum to other Hong Kong people. So, he felt that it was a lot of struggling to seek asylum in the United Kingdom because he wanted to stay loyal to Hong Kong; but he also presented that asking the United Kingdom to grant asylum to other Hong Kong people is for their benefit …

Nathan Law continues his fund-raising campaigns by declaring to be fighting for Hong Kong pro-democracy or pro-independence movements when he is in the United Kingdom. Despite he was benefited from the democratic movement by gaining a Master Degree from Yale University, he asks for similar amounts of donations compared to Ted Hui. So, do not worry about his livelihoods.

https://www.patreon.com/nathanlaw

The most pathetic was his mother. Nathan Law in the United Kingdom publicly announced that he was 'forced' to terminate his relationship with his single mother as he became wanted by the Hong Kong police. So, Joshua Wong's parents got into the plane through Hong Kong customs and were granted entrance to Australia for having a pro-democracy son. And Nathan Law's mother was abandoned by his son because she has a pro-democracy son. Everything is the fault of the Chinese government!! Some believe Nathan Law just did not want to support his mother and used the Hong Kong government's prosecution as his excuse. Poor thing, his Chinese mother raised him and his siblings as his father divorced her early.

https://tw.news.yahoo.com/%E7%BE%85%E5%86%A0%E8%81%B0%E5%B0%88%E8%A8%AA3-%E6%84%A7%E5%B0%8D%E6%AF%8D%E8%A6%AA%E8%A2%AB%E8%BF%AB%E6%96%B7%E7%B5%95%E9%97%9C%E4%BF%82-%E6%88%91%E5%9C%A8%E8%B5%B0%E4%B8%8D%E7%9F%A5%E5%A6%82%E4%BD%95%E5%9B%9E%E5%A0%B1%E5%AE%B6%E4%BA%BA%E7%9A%84%E8%B7%AF-215857670.html

In 2021 mother's day, Nathan Law posted his old photo with his mother, showing his supporters how much he missed and loved his mother.

If he did miss his mother, he would have shown his love to his mother, not to his Internet followers. After terminating his relationship with his mother, he was still using her. Sad!

Nathan Law's mother had not spoken to the press since his son announced 'being forced' to terminate their relationship. It was the divorced single mother who used to support him in front of the public when he was sentenced to prison. You can tell how sad the wordless single mother now is.

Talking about parents, you may ask why Nathan Law needs asylum in the United Kingdom? Now the United Kingdom has opened their door to BNO holders who was born in Hong Kong when it was a British colony before 1997. According to Wiki, Nathan Law was born in 1993 in Shenzhen, China. Nathan has a Hong Kong father and a Mainland Chinese mother. He moved to Hong Kong with his mother for a family reunion when he was around six.

Nathan Law is Chinese and was born in China. Unlike most other Hong Kong citizens who were born in Hong Kong or their parents were, Nathan Law is therefore not qualified for the offer.

L10. Democracy and Finance? Donation scandals

Under COVID-19, Chief Executive Carrie Lam announced that all senior government officers reduce their salary by 10% to save taxpayers money. There was a discussion about whether senators in the Legislative Council should also reduce their salaries.

The leader of the pro-democracy Hong Kong Civic Party at that time, Alvin Yeung Ngok-kiu was one of the senators. He said, 'We believe the **principal goal of donation is to support the 'yellow (i.e., pro-democracy)' trading circle.** 我哋認為捐助的首要任務係支持黃色經濟圈'

https://www.youtube.com/watch?v=j0laPPEx2B4 (0:00-0:05)

https://www.singtao.ca/4196357/2020-04-09/news-楊岳橋%3A公民黨議員擬捐薪予「黃色經濟圈」/?variant=zh-hk

In Hong Kong's recent democratic movements, 'democracy' is often linked to the economy or trading. In 2020, I received a Facebook post by my former teacher in Hong Kong, stating 'There is a COVID-19 case in L Y Estate. A pro-democracy restaurant there is losing businesses. * Siblings, please go to support the pro-democracy restaurant there!' (Hong Kong pro-democracy protesters call each other 'siblings' or 'righteous heroes')

Under COVID-19, shouldn't everyone avoid moving around and avoid going to hotspots to reduce the spread of the virus? But it is the idea of this so-called democratic movement: If you are pro-democracy, then protesters are encouraged to support your business and your livelihood. If you are not democratic, then protesters should avoid supporting your restaurants.

Furthermore, quite a lot of businesses were attacked due to their Chinese background or just due to their supporting the government and police.

After the announcement of the new national security law, the United Kingdom has opened their doors to Hong Kong people who were born when it was a British colony. Anecdotally, the Hong Kong new migrants in parts of the United Kingdom have asked shops to declare going against the Chinese government and Hong Kong government, or they would face boycotts by the pro-democracy Hong Kong asylum seekers. (Being asylum seekers does not mean they are poor. They usually sell their property in Hong Kong and bring along with a vast fund, as Hong Kong property prices have raised a few times in recent years.)

However, in front of foreigners, they say the opposite way. In Joshua Wong and Denise Ho's presentation of their case before a congressional commission for requesting U.S. sanctions against China and Hong Kong, they said, 'Beijing shouldn't have it both ways, reaping all the economic benefits of Hong Kong's standing in the world while eradicating our freedoms.'

https://www.washingtonpost.com/world/asia_pacific/hong-kong-activists-press-us-to-counter-chinas-erosion-of-citys-freedoms/2019/09/17/99a7d542-d8fb-11e9-a1a5-162b8a9c9ca2_story.html

So, in Joshua Wong's opinion, Hong Kong is asking for freedom because of the economic benefits it has given to China? So, human rights and freedom are only for those with money????? No money, no democracy?????

And it also demonstrates their lack of understanding of economies in the region. When Hong Kong first returned to China in 1997, many Hong Kong people had become enthusiastic about taking advantage of China's rapidly growing economy. Entrepreneurs, actors/actresses and working professionals in Hong Kong including myself were interested to gain some Chinese exposure and reap the economic benefits when Hong Kong started a close relationship with China. Around 2014, many top offices in central districts of Hong Kong were occupied by the wealthiest companies from China. In contrast, top foreign companies moved out from the most expensive offices to the less expensive ones in regional areas of Hong Kong.

My ex-colleagues in multi-national companies were kind of disappointed to be moved to 2nd class offices.

Furthermore, Hong Kong, being a part of China, has been enjoying the privilege of much lower tax rates compared to other parts of China. Refer to my book 1, *Hong Kong Protest Leaders - Sick Facts that Western countries do not know*.

Joshua Wong had always been a full-time student in political studies and public administration in a bottom university, then a full-time organizer of his political party (which he said he earned no salary from there but has been living wealthily). Denise Ho has always been a full-time musician and only have a diploma in Arts and Communications. You cannot blame them for knowing nothing about economies.

In this so-called democratic movement, the activists somehow believe that sanctions against their own country will bring democracy. In 2020, I even received an Internet poll to request U.S. sanctions against the Hong Kong government!

Like many other Hongkongers, in the financial hub, gains in the stock market was one of my income sources. Sanctions toward Hong Kong and China will definitely harm the economy of the people and have little threat to the sovereignty of the government. Under a poor economy, civilians must suffer. But it was what the so-called Hong Kong Democrats say would help Hong Kong getting more democracy and human rights.

Not only so, but the so-called 'Hong Kong Democrats' had also requested the United States to force Hong Kong goods to be labelled as 'Made in China' instead of 'Made in Hong Kong'. Hong Kong goods have always been reputable about their good quality and have been priced higher than the cheap Chinese goods. The so-called 'Hong Kong Democrats' had also requested Donald Trump to remove Hong Kong's special trading status. They believe by damaging Hong Kong's brands, it will gain democracy and human rights.

So, what is this so-called democratic movement is all about? Are the 'Hong Kong Democrats' unhappy about the 1 country 2 systems policy and want to make it a 1 country 1 system? While they complain about the disappearing 1 country 2 systems, they are urging to turn it into 1 country 1 system!

https://www.scmp.com/economy/china-economy/article/3119193/us-rejects-hong-kong-request-wto-panel-over-made-china

Talking about money. When you read Chapter L6 the enormous money Jimmy Lai had donated to different democratic parties and pro-democracy activists, you will probably know that Jimmy Lai is only one of their sources of income. They would probably have been receiving money from many others.

In Hong Kong's democratic movement, activists can easily receive large amounts of donations either locally or from overseas. Joshua Wong was only an example of a wealthy activist allegedly living on donations from the public. There had also long been accusations by Chinese officials that Joshua Wong and many other activists have been financially supported by the United States, namely the National Endowment for Democracy (NEC).

https://today.line.me/hk/v2/article/5nrQXv

Joshua Wong had denied this accusation. Same as he had denied getting money from public donations for his personal use. If both his statements are true, his wealth would be totally unexplainable.

In fact, there had long been multiple accusations that foreign powers have been conspiracy funding the Hong Kong Democrats for pro-independence and anti-government movements. They aim to use the fight for 'democracy' and 'human rights' as a cover-up to gradually lead the people to anti-Chinese and pro-independence movements. Joshua Wong was not the only one alleged to have a close relationship with the United States or European political leaders, some others such as

Hong Kong Alliance in Support of Patriotic Democratic Movements of China was allegedly receiving donations from the United States too. Are these true or not? I do not know. For these, the organization is currently under investigation under the new national security law. Some of their leaders, such as Albert Ho Chun-Yan and Lee Cheuk Yan were alleged to have a close relationship with the United States or European countries too. Once again, I do not know whether these are true or not.

http://www.takungpao.com.hk/news/232109/2021/0821/622788.html

And one does not need to be as famous as Joshua Wong to gain donations for the democratic movements. The idea of 'international frontline' has been advocated by Hong Kong's opposition in recent years since the mid-2010s. Since the new national security law was in effect in June 2020, many activists go into exile abroad. They then say their exiles is an effective way 'international frontline' to convince foreign governments where they are in to support Hong Kong independence or impose sanctions against the Chinese and Hong Kong governments for the sake of enhancing its human rights and democracy.

Obvious examples were Wong (the fake Han 韓寶生) and Ted Hui in earlier chapters who both asked for donations to support his Hong Kong movement while going into exile in the United Kingdom. (Ted Hui was also in the United Kingdom when he first asked for donations from his Hong Kong supporters. He is now in Australia.)

Let us watch Ted Hui's Facebook post to ask for Hong Kong people's donation while he was in the United Kingdom (probably he has been rejected asylum in the United Kingdom and later entered Australia). 'Patreon' is a platform for many Hong Kong activists including Ted Hui, Nathan Law and Joshua Wong to receive donations.

https://www.facebook.com/permalink.php?story_fbid=16893778 77911068&id=178843345631203&_cft_[0]=AZV9Phjt37KH56 ttgHrzR1voTucqT50CK-o1PCrPYjyCnhOU9WDwAAPs7f73cg5730sWBFNdkNc5t7vjVQ cvc0RZDcNGD_tKbw6UuAsn4swM2VYOtrUSgYJiVii1dY_PleJ 1nqPKMZhvWZdhwV-CAxvzKXtB-XqJIxfpdRnAl9LriXeDTROsnU23nvL9Aee948U&_tn_=%2C O%2CP-R

He advertised on his Facebook post: 'After a lot of struggling in my heart, I finally open an account on Patreon. The first time I was asked why I do not open a Patreon account was a year ago. Now, more and more politicians (from Hong Kong) have opened Patreon, and more people are asking me to do it too. **Many civilians say they wish to give me donations** but they did not know how to. I did not previously open a Patreon account (until now) for a few reasons. First, I had been a senator in Hong Kong for a few terms and I did have enough money for living. **I felt uneasy to ask for donations**. 經內心一番拉扯，我終於開啟了 Patreon。還記得第一次被問起為何不開 Patreon，應該是超過一年前了。直至最近，身邊越來越多政治人物都開了 Patreon，我就被問得更多，市民總對我說 "想課金支持你，但無途徑啊"，然後我總一笑置之。其實我一直不肯開 Patreon，有幾個原因。第一，我做了超過兩屆區議員及一屆立法會議員，期間是有議員酬金及營運開支津貼償還。生計不是問題，又有團隊幫忙，為何仍要公眾課金支持呢？自己總過意不去。'

And sarcastically, he was exactly asking for donations when he said these.

His post continues with his justification for his fund-raising, 'Now that I am in exile abroad. There is only one thing I must do for the rest of my life – Resurrect Hong Kong (or translate it as 'make Hong Kong independent')! Have a good fight in the 'international frontline'. Although I am now in a foreign country, I have never worried about my livelihoods. I am confident I can do whatever works and see no difficulty in feeding my family. However, after a lot of thinking, if I can continue to work as a full-time politician, concentrating in the work on the 'international frontline', I can surely do more for Hong Kong. Thus, I now fearfully open a Patreon account (to receive donations). 如今我流亡海外，餘生只有一件事要做好：為光復香港，打好國際戰線。雖然人在海外，但其實我從無擔心過生計，亦有自信可應付各類型工作，養起自己一家人總不困難。但我仔細思量，若我可像以往一樣全職作為一個從政者，全心專注國際戰線的工作，能為香港做到的事必定更多。現在戰戰兢兢開啟 Patreon …'

Now, going into exile as an asylum seeker is more profitable than ever. From what he said above, instead of going to work, he would like to be a 'full-time politician' for Hong Kong when he is in the United Kingdom (or Australia). Perhaps he wants his supporters to believe he would have meetings with the British/Australian Prime Minister every day? And if no one is willing to meet with him, then he can go for a pay leave every day. Or maybe he plans to use the donations to put on advertisements in foreign newspapers to request sanctions against the Hong Kong government like Jimmy Lai did? Sorry, no! Ted Hui had promised that the donations are used to support him (as his salary) as a full-time politician.

After the 2019-20 riots, many pro-democracy Hong Kong civilians had moved to the United Kingdom as asylum seekers. Many were previously middle class and now became grassroots in the United Kingdom due to un-proficient English skills, lack of relationship networks and less recognized education or qualifications in a foreign country. In contrast, Ted Hui secures his salary as a 'full-time politician' working using people's donations while he is in the United Kingdom/Australia. What a contrast! Well, he does have an obvious difference from other civilians who become grassroots after they migrate to foreign countries - Ted Hui is an official criminal with many different criminal charges with solid evidence.

Ted Hui's face always makes me think of Frederick Chong the scammer in my book, *I'm a Romance Scam IT Detective*. Maybe their personalities or natures are too similar.

Want to support Ted Hui the criminal seeking asylum in Australia? Here is his donation platform:

https://www.patreon.com/tedhui

Even Joshua Wong in jail continues to receive donations. Right before he went to jail, he had reminded his supporters to subscribe to make regular donations to him:

https://www.patreon.com/joshuawong

Comparing the amounts of donations they are asking for, Joshua Wong is asking for double to 8 times the amounts. And because he is famous internationally, he probably gets 4-8 times what Ted Hui gets. Considering Ted Hui asks for donations as his salary as a full-time politician, and that Joshua Wong is expected to get at least 2-8 times more. **Joshua Wong in prison can easily be gaining a lot more income than yours plus mine.**

Don't worry. As of today, Joshua Wong does not have sufficient charges to get life imprisonment. He will probably be released in 10 years and enjoy the rest of his life with the fund he now gains.

So, on the one hand, protest leaders urge the people to sacrifice Hong Kong's economy for the sake of the fight for democracy; on the other hand, they urge the people to pay them money to support them.

Some Hongkongers call these people 'political scammers 政棍'.

(It is important to know that paying donations to fund the works of secession or requesting foreign interference may be sufficient to violate the national security law. Especially, as of the time of writing, Ted Hui's donation link had emphasized the donation was to fund his work to convince foreign interference into Hong Kong's matter. Ted Hui's donation link claims that the donation platform 'is not Hong Kong-based and donators' personal information will be kept secret'.

In fact, the Internet is not as safe as he thinks. Or, maybe he knows the Internet is not as safe, but he pretends he does not know and let his supporters in Hong Kong risk violating the law paying him donations?)

Look at Sonia Ng's example in Chapter F2, the fake Han 韓寶生, the pro-democracy restaurant in L Y Estate, and the wealthy Joshua Wong and full-time retiree Ted Hui in Australia. **Isn't it right to say that this 'democratic movement' is even more communist than the communist Chinese government?** When they do not have jobs or they have less official income than other pro-democracy 'siblings' (or they present so), they just ask other pro-democracy 'siblings' to share money with them by donating money.

Even Chinese communists had improved a lot over the last few decades and do not do this anymore!

It was reported that even some with hidden identities have gained impressive donations for claiming to act on the democratic movements.

https://hk.on.cc/hk/bkn/cnt/commentary/20201122/mobile/bkn-20201122000415576-1122_00832_001.html

Let us look into some un-anonymous cases. This former primary school teacher was convicted for assaulting a police officer(s). He asked for donations on the Internet for taking care of his parents when he went to jail and soon gained HKD 5,000,000 (USD 643,500). He did not disclose the fact that he and his family have 2 properties worth over HKD 13,000,000 (USD 1,673,000) when he asked for donations.

https://hkgpao.com/articles/1017144

He was soon arrested for possible money laundering. If you have read my book, *I'm a Romance Scam IT Detective: Psychological Games * Real IT Analysis * Legal Matters*, you probably remember banks are legally obligated to monitor transactions and report suspicious ones to the authority, who may ask their police to investigate. This applies to most, if not all, of the countries in the world.

Now, look at more famous ones. Do you remember the 'Hong Kong twelve' who were arrested by the Chinese customs for mistakenly entering the Chinese sea when they attempted to escape to Taiwan? A few of them had already pleaded guilty to their violent crimes after being arrested by China and sent back to Hong Kong. Amongst them, 17-year-old Wong Fuk-lam, had revealed that some had not only arranged a 'safe' place for him to stay but also donated HKD 150,000 (USD 19300) to pay for his exile expenses.

In July 2021, there was a bomb creation case in Hong Kong you may have watched on International news. 3 high school students aged 17, 19 and 15 were paid to create and place bombs for the fight for Hong Kong independence. 14 people were arrested, in which a few of them are payers of the bomb attack. Payers include a university staff member, a high school teacher and a property manager in an entertainment giant. Employers of these payers of the attack, including the university and the entertainment giant, have fired them.

https://www.ettoday.net/news/20210708/2025891.htm

* Since the 2019 democratic movements, those who support the protests have called each other 'righteous heroes'(義士) or 'siblings' (手足). It is because the protesters feel that a fight for democracy is righteous. They call each other 'siblings' as they believe they support each other as much as brothers and sisters.

In contrast, those who are against the protests have started to call themselves 'normally people 正常人'. It was because they feel it is normal to obey laws and orders.

Hong Kong Protest Leaders - Sick Facts that Western Countries do not know 2

Hong Kong national security law – cases, regulations, rules ...

N1. Myths …

According to Joshua Wong in an interview with Australia's SBS news in around July 2020, he said that he could be charged under the new national security law merely for speaking in that interview with foreign TV news. However, after a year, he eventually was not charged for the interview.

There have been so many rumours about the new national security law. So, what can make one get arrested? And how can you ensure you will not be arrested? Most of the foreign press has been emphasizing that the maximum penalty of the new national security law is life imprisonment. But does it mean one can easily get life imprisonment for any violation of Hong Kong national security law? And is the penalty heavier, compared to the national security laws of other countries? Let us look into different cases and the actual law in this section.

N2. Secession: Hong Kong independence?

The first man officially charged under the new national security law was Tong Ying-kit, a civilian. Just 1 day after the new national security law was imposed, he drove a motorbike to hit 3 police officers with a protest flag of '光復香港, 時代革命 Liberate Hong Kong. Revolution of our times.' (It is important to understand that the Chinese slogan does not match the English slogan. To learn what his Chinese slogan actually means, refer to my book 1, *Hong Kong Protest Leaders - Sick Facts that Western countries do not know*).

At a glance, he was sentenced to 9 years in prison for the violation of the new national security law. But it is very important to note that his sentence for terrorism alone was 8 years. The majority of his imprisonment of terrorism and violation of national security law overlap, with only 2.5 years run consecutively. That means even if the new national security law were not in effect, he would still have been sentenced to 8 years imprisonment for injuring the 3 police officers and dangerous driving (more explanation below). **Although he was officially sentenced for secession with 6.5 years' imprisonment, the crime of secession only added 1 year to his actual jail term.**

https://www.smh.com.au/world/asia/hong-kong-waiter-sentenced-to-nine-years-in-jail-under-security-law-20210730-p58ef3.html

Tong's lawyer said that they would appeal both the conviction and the sentence. His lawyer emphasized that the crime of secession should only bring him less than 5 years in jail. As for his hitting police officers with the motorbike, his lawyer said he was 'not intentional' and the police officers were 'not severely injured' and should only bring him 3 to 10 years jail term. We will see how the appeal goes.

https://www.rfi.fr/cn/%E6%B8%AF%E6%BE%B3%E5%8F%B0/20210730-%E9%A6%99%E6%B8%AF%E5%9C%8B%E5%AE%89%E6%B3%95%E9%A6%96%E6%A1%88%E5%94%90%E8%8B%B1%E5%82%91%E8%A2%AB%E5%88%A49%E5%B9%B4-%E5%BE%8B%E5%B8%AB-%E5%B0%87%E4%B8%8A%E8%A8%B4

Was he not intentional? Decide it yourself by re-visiting how he crashed into the policemen:

https://www.youtube.com/watch?v=c2fId3Kkpk4

From his case, you can see that **Hong Kong lawyers and the Hong Kong community generally agree that the new national security law would, most of the time, only jail the convicted a few years, not the 'life imprisonment'** that foreign critics have been emphasizing. (You will understand more when we compare with the United States below).

From the same report, please note that many civilians were in the court screaming to support Tong, 'I support you, Tong!', 'Be strong, Tong!' and 'Innocent are those who fight (against the government)!' None of these supporters was arrested for supporting him or for saying these in the public. **It is not as easy to get arrested under the new national security law.**

However, in Tong's case, the judges had decided that the Chinese slogan in 2019 protests '光復香港, 時代革命' violates the national security law under the crime of secession because it advocates Hong Kong independence. It becomes a case law for anyone using this Chinese slogan in the future. Anyone using this Chinese slogan can be convicted for secession. **But it is important to remember that their English slogan 'Free Hong Kong' or 'Liberate Hong Kong. Revolution of our times.' does not match this Chinese slogan that protesters usually put together as if they are related.** (Refer to my book 1, *Hong Kong Protest Leaders - Sick Facts that Western countries do not know*). Therefore, saying the English slogan 'Liberate Hong Kong' and 'Free Hong Kong' without putting the mismatched Chinese slogan is unlikely to put one in jail.

In the hearing, one of the major topics the lawyers debated on was whether his Chinese slogan 光復香港 means Hong Kong independence or not. This indicated whether he would be convicted for secession or not. No one seemed to bother to discuss the English slogan 'liberate Hong Kong' in the hearing as it was not a matter of concern.

The lawyers had quoted a lot of previous usages of the words '光復' from a lot of literary sources to debate whether '光復' implies secession or independence (香港 = Hong Kong). However, I believe it is important for me to share with you my understanding of the word '光復' as a layman in literature because the national security law applies to everyone including laymen – as you know, I studied science and am a layman in literature. In book 1, I have explained the literary meaning of the word '光復', where this word does not have an explicit meaning of 'independency' or 'secession'. **However, in terms of usage, '光復' is indeed often about a 'change of sovereignty'.** Let us look into a famous historical case that everyone in Hong Kong knows: the cleverest man in Chinese History, Zhuge Liang, had advocated '興復漢室' in his writing. He referred to taking China's sovereigns from Cao Cao's hand back to the Han kingdom (漢室). Some also called '興復漢室' as '光復漢室'. Here, '光復' does mean a change of sovereignty.

https://kknews.cc/history/4b352ng.html

In the court, lawyers had used few other examples of usage of the words that we laymen are not that familiar with. Anyway, the court had accepted that '光復香港' means Hong Kong independence and thus secession.

N3. Terrorism: what are the international standards?

Now, let us look into the sentence of terrorism in his case. Yes, officially, Hong Kong did not have laws against terrorism before the new national security law was in effect on June 30, 2020. However, practically, before that date, terrorism was judged under other criminal laws including Offences against the Person Ordinance, the Firearms and Ammunition Ordinance and Organized and Serious Crimes Ordinance. **The highest penalty for the Offences against Person Ordinance or the Firearms and Ammunition Ordinance has been life imprisonment.** The highest penalty for the Organized and Serious Crimes Ordinance is 14 years behind bars and HKD 5,000,000 (USD 643,500). Therefore, the new national security law against terrorism has not increased the jail terms for the same crimes.

Researching the United Nation's website, while it has a lot of publications on what they do to counter-terrorism, I could not find any documents giving definitions of 'terrorism':

https://www.un.org/counterterrorism/about

According to multiple government websites across the world (the below website is Arizona Department of Emergency and Military Affairs), it states, '**The UN Member States still have no agreed-upon definition of terrorism**'.

https://dema.az.gov/sites/default/files/Publications/AR-Terrorism%20Definitions-BORUNDA.pdf

The same document also clarified the definition of 'terrorism' in the United States is '…activities that involve violent … or life-threatening acts … that are a violation of the criminal laws of the United States or any State and … appear to be intended (i) to intimidate or coerce a civilian population; (ii) to influence the policy of a government by intimidation or coercion; or (iii) to affect the conduct of a government by mass destruction, assassination, or kidnapping; and…(C) occur primarily within the territorial jurisdiction of the United States…'

From here, Hong Kong Tong Ying-kit's attack and Benny Tai's '10 steps to die/lose together' do match all the definitions by the United States, except that it occurs in Hong Kong (instead of the United States).

The Hong Kong government had also justified its new national security law by comparing them with other countries' in the world. 'On advocating terrorism, no one could use freedom of speech, of publication or the press, etc, as an excuse to advocate or defend terrorist activities and such beliefs or theories, and must not promote or cheer for the mutual destruction slogans and propositions that would endanger the safety of public lives and properties or disrupt public order. In fact, many countries such as the United Kingdom, Australia and France have already put in place relevant laws to prohibit advocating or glorifying terrorism.'

https://www.news.gov.hk/eng/2021/07/20210710/20210710_121147_433.html

N4. Details of Hong Kong national security law: protection of human rights, publishments and scope of power

Under Hong Kong's new national security law, there are four types of crimes:

1) secession,
2) subversion of state power,
3) terrorist activities
4) collusion with foreign or external powers to endanger national security

https://www.isd.gov.hk/nationalsecurity/eng/pdf/NSL_QnA_Book.pdf

This government booklet introduces the background to the enactment of the new national security law in Hong Kong SAR. It outlines the main content and answers some common questions in respect of the Law. It has clearly specified why the law is necessary, and how it intends to protect people's human rights and freedom of speech (P.12).

It started by displaying photos of explosives found in 2019-20 riots (P.8) and protesters' clashing into the Legislative Council and damaging facilities there (P.10). (Also refers to Chapter L7.) It clarifies the government's dedication to guarantee fair trials, the presumption of innocence and no retrospective power (P.14). It emphasizes that the **Hong Kong Basic Law (article #23) stipulates that Hong Kong shall enact laws on its own to prohibit seven types of acts and activities that endanger national security.** And the new national security law is the enactment of such legislation (P.21).

Hong Kong is not a nation. Under one country, two systems, Hong Kong's nation is China. As such, Hong Kong has no power to decide its 'national' security law on behalf of the Chinese Nation.

And given so many countries including Australia, United States and the United Kingdom have their own national security law, it is really not wrong for China to implement it in its territory, Hong Kong. If western countries feel that the law is a crackdown on human rights and democracy, then these countries should first abolish their national security laws.

Sadly, foreigners generally are confused and believe Hong Kong is a fully independent jurisdiction. Foreign critics and politicians criticise the law because it was the Chinese leaders who decide the legislations of the law, bypassing the Hong Kong Legislative Council and Hong Kong government. In fact, according to the Sino-British Joint Declaration signed by the British and the Chinese leaders, Hong Kong is supposed to be under one country, two systems, which promises a high degree of autonomy under the Chinese's reign, not complete autonomy. Under Hong Kong's basic law, the Chinese government has absolute sovereignty over Hong Kong. Unfortunately, many foreigners feel that China has invaded Hong Kong by enforcing the law without passing the local government. It is a complete misunderstanding in the Sino-British Joint Declaration and one country, two systems.

Now, let us look at the details of Hong Kong's national security law. Unfortunately, it does not seem to have an English version. Probably because the targets are either Hong Kong people or Chinese people.

https://www.elegislation.gov.hk/hk/A406

Under national security law regulation #22 and #23, anyone who incites, helps and use money and other valuable to support secession or subversion of state power. For lighter cases, he/she will be jailed for less than 5 years. For more severe cases, he/she can be jailed for 5 years to 10 years.

In Chapter N7, you will see which activists are likely to be convicted.

The national security law has also specified its scope of power. Under regulation #36, it applies to anyone in Hong Kong. It also applies when one of the actions or the consequences happen in Hong Kong.

Regulation #37: the law applies to Hong Kong permanent residents, companies and legal entities incorporated in Hong Kong. It also applies to non-legal entities organizations established outside Hong Kong.

Under regulation #38: the law also applies to individuals who do not have Hong Kong permanent residency and commit the crime outside Hong Kong.

Under regulation #39: the law only applies to actions performed after the law was in effect (i.e., June 30, 2020 evening).

Some Hong Kong critics said that the penalties of Hong Kong's national security law are not actually as heavy, compared to other countries. According to their research, the highest penalty of treason in the United States of America is the death penalty. In contrast, Hong Kong's highest penalty of treason is only a life sentence. Let us look at their government website:

https://uscode.house.gov/view.xhtml?path=/prelim@title18/part1/chapter115&edition=prelim

And the Hong Kong government emphasized that the four types of offence set out under the NSL (national security law) are similar to those in foreign countries. Some countries vest more drastic powers in their law enforcement agencies than those in Hong Kong under the NSL. A speaker even pointed out that there is a country which could put people, who are suspected of endangering national security, in detention without charge for two years.

https://www.news.gov.hk/eng/2021/07/20210710/20210710_121147_433.html

N5. Subversion of the Chinese government; Rules on granting bail

In the 35+ election, 47 Democrats in Hong Kong were arrested for supporting Benny Tai's '10 steps to die/lose together 攬炒十步'. There, steps 7, 9 and 10 in the plan were to paralyse the Hong Kong government and ultimately make foreign countries impose sanctions against the Chinese/Hong Kong governments. They were charged under subversion of the Chinese sovereignty under the new national security law.

Under Hong Kong's national security law regulation #22.3, 'severely interfere, stop or damage the Chinese government organizations or Hong Kong's sovereignty organizations from performing its duties', Benny Tai's explicit plan was to paralyse the Hong Kong government from functioning had obviously violated this law.

While the hearings were still proceeding, 15 of the arrested were granted bail and the other 32 were refused bail. The court considered the severity of their crime to be different. According to a Hong Kong pro-government politician who studied law, the national security law has a guideline on different levels of punishments depending on the levels of involvement of the convicted. 'For those who participate in 35+, as they are only participants, the jail terms for subversion of the sovereignty would be less than 3 years. For those who actively participated in it, their jail terms would be 3 to 10 years. But those who initiated it and urged others to join it can be jailed for over 10 years. Benny Tai and Claudia Mo are expected to fall into this category.'

Refer to regulation #23.

Even for such a large-scale and explicit subversion, no one is likely to be sentenced to life imprisonment.

According to regulation #43 of the national security law, the judge can grant bail to suspects and defendants if there are sufficient reasons to believe he/she would not continue to implement further damages to the national security.

N6. Elections and national security law

Talking about elections, the national security law was prophetical. Regulation #35 states, 'Anyone who was decided by the court that has violated the national security law would lose his/her position as candidates in the Legislative Council election, District Council election or the Chief Executive Election. Anyone who has vowed or declared supporting Hong Kong Basic Law and being loyal to the Chinese Communists' Hong Kong Special Administrative Region (HKSAR) as a lawmaker in Legislative Council, a government officer or a public servant (and have been decided by the court that has violated the national security law) would immediately lose their positions.'

Therefore, sounds like anyone in 35+, if convicted, would lose their eligibility to run the election as a lawmaker in the Legislative Council or becomes a candidate as the Chief Executive.

Actually, this rule is not new. **The rule has always been here before the imposing of the new national security law.**

Look at Chow Ting's case in 2018-19, she was originally disqualified (DQ) as a candidate in the Legislative Council election. The reason for her disqualification was that 'self-determination', her political party's election promise, was widely considered to refer to 'Hong Kong independence'. According to the court, 'Hong Kong independency' is considered to have violated Hong Kong Basic Law article #1 'Hong Kong is a part of China'. Therefore, Chow Ting was considered 'not supporting Hong Kong Basic Law' and was disqualified under Hong Kong Basic Law, article #104, which requires every lawmaker in the Legislative Council or similar needs to vow to defend Hong Kong Basic Law.

Agnes Chow's appeal to the High Court in September 2019 was successful, only because the election officer had made a procedural mistake. The High Court said, 'The election officer should have given Agnes Chow a chance to explain, defend herself and try to convince the election officer to change his/her mind.' The High Court said that a person's right to be elected should be protected.

However, the High Court did emphasize that Hong Kong is a part of China under Hong Kong Basic Law, which has been in effect since Hong Kong returned to China in July 1997. Therefore, anyone advocating Hong Kong independence or 'Hong Kong self-determination' would be considered as objecting to the Basic Law and the Hong Kong government.

The High Court said that if the election officer had given Chow Ting a chance to explain and defend herself and that the election officer had made the same decision (to disqualify her), then the High Court would not have overridden the election officer's decision.

https://hongkongfp.com/2019/09/02/breaking-judge-overturns-govt-decision-ban-hong-kong-activist-agnes-chow-election/

From this case, you can see that the law to disqualify anyone who supports Hong Kong independence or 'Hong Kong self-determination' has always existed under the Basic Law since Hong Kong returned to China in July 1997.

The point is that, in the 35+ election, so many Democrats had chosen the path vow to paralyse the Hong Kong government and initiate foreign sanctions against their own government. It had never happened in such a large-scale and explicit way.

Without the new national security law, then each of these Democrats has always needed to go through the process of convincing the election officers that they truly support the Hong Kong Basic Law. If they are considered to advocate Hong Kong independence or plan to paralyse the Hong Kong government or society, it has always been sufficient to get them disqualified.

Now, with the national security law in place, once they have got determined by the court that they had violated the national security law, they would naturally be disqualified.

Same results.

N7. Collusion with foreign or external powers to endanger national security

For Jimmy Lai's case, as we have discussed in Chapter L6, he is charged under the new national security law for asking foreign governments, foreign organizations and officers to impose sanctions against the Hong Kong government and the Chinese government in a large number of articles in his Apple Daily since the new national security law was imposed on June 30, 2020. Within Apple Daily, only 5 company directors who are the final decision-makers on the contents of these articles have been arrested. No other former employees of Apple Daily had been arrested under the national security law.

On the other hand, the convicted Andy Li and Chan Tsz-wah had already become state witnesses against Jimmy Lai and his right-hand man Mark Simon (Refer to Chapter L6). One cannot say Jimmy Lai was arrested for no solid evidence.

N8. Pleading guilty? Reducing publishment?

At the moment, we can only have a brief look at the first case of pleading guilty to the national security law. As mentioned in Chapter L6, Andy Li and Chan Tsz-wah had pleaded guilty to foreign collusion and are still waiting for the sentence. As a usual practice, pleading guilty to criminal crimes in Hong Kong normally reduce the sentence by one-third. Does it apply to national security law too?

Officially, under #32, offenders who proactively surrender to the police would get lighter penalties. And for those who expose their syndicates, if found to be real, their penalties would also be reduced. Those who are self-initiated to stop the execution of the crime would also get reduced penalties or even be avoided any penalties.

As Andy Li and Chan Tsz-wah had actually committed the crimes, despite pleading guilty, they are still likely to be sentenced to certain penalties. But it is expected to be lighter than those who do not plead guilty. It also depends on whether their accusations against their alleged syndicates, Jimmy Lai and Mark Simon, are found to be real or not.

Therefore, it is still important to look at the evidence. Refer to Chapter L6, in one of the marketing events alone, Jimmy Lai first paid HKD 1,500,000 (USD 193,000) to put on advertisements by Andy Li in foreign newspapers against the Chinese and Hong Kong government and expected later reimbursement from the public donations that Andy Li would organize. Young civilian like Andy Li is unlikely to have such funds without the help of Jimmy Lai or other tycoons. Thus, his source of funds may be able to prove Jimmy Lai's involvement in this case. Of course, we can tell when Jimmy Lai attends hearings about this charge.

N9. Advocators who glorify and encourage suicide attacks without doing it themselves

We had talked about cases that criminals proactively involve in terrorism, seeking foreign sanctions against their own government and subversion of the Chinese or Hong Kong's sovereignty. But what about those who encourage other people to do these without doing it themselves? Refer to the last chapter, it is very prevalent for those self-proclaimed 'pro-democracy activists' to urge others to break the law without themselves breaking these laws.

On July 1, 2021, there was a suicide attack against policemen in Causeway Bay, Hong Kong. While the majority of the Hong Kong society was furious about the terrorist attack, few rare Hong Kong locals, namely a university student union, publicly praise the man in the suicide attack and 'thanked' him for his 'sacrifice for Hong Kong' 感激梁為香港作出的犧牲 in their university magazine.

https://www.aljazeera.com/news/2021/7/2/hong-kong-officer-stabbed-by-lone-wolf-attacker-security-chief

https://std.stheadline.com/daily/article/2373857/%E6%97%A5%E5%A0%B1-%E6%B8%AF%E8%81%9E-%E6%B8%AF%E5%A4%A7%E5%AD%B8%E7%94%9F%E9%9C%83%E8%A9%95%E8%AD%B0%E6%9C%83%E6%82%BC%E5%88%BA%E8%AD%A6%E5%85%87%E5%BE%92-%E6%A0%A1%E6%96%B9%E8%AD%B4%E8%B2%AC?fb_comment_id=3867170673409918_3867880073338978

The student union was condemned by their university and many others in the society for praising and encouraging suicide attacks and terrorism. Facing the threat of being expelled from the university, all members of this student union 'withdraw' their speech and 'apologized' to the public. They also resigned from their positions in the student union. However, many believe they did not sincerely repent. One of the reasons was what was written on the back of their clothes when they apologized to the public. And many criticized that no matter if their repent were sincere or not, it would not change what they had done wrong in the first place. One cannot just say something very wrong and then 'withdraws' and 'apologies' as if nothing has ever happened.

1.5 months later, in August 2021, 4 of the members of the student union was charged under national security law #27 'promoting terrorism or inciting implementation of terrorist activities'. They were also charged with 'inciting others to injure people 煽惑他人有意圖而傷人的交替控罪'. The police did not rule out the possibility that more people involved in the case would be arrested. https://news.tvb.com/local/611e2ef834b0316d729bc2d6/%E5%9B%9B%E6%B8%AF%E5%A4%A7%E7%94%9F%E8%A2%AB%E6%8E%A7%E5%AE%A3%E6%8F%9A%E6%81%90%E6%80%96%E4%B8%BB%E7%BE%A9%E7%BD%AA-%E8%A5%BF%E4%B9%9D%E9%BE%8D%E8%A3%81%E5%88%A4%E6%B3%95%E9%99%A2%E6%8F%90%E5%A0%82

According to Hong Kong's national security law #27, for more serious cases, one can be jailed for 5-10 years with fines, or possibly the confiscation of property. However, these 4 people are unlikely to be considered as very serious cases because their speech has not directly led to more terrorist attacks, at least not yet or not identified yet. Therefore, they are likely to be jailed under 5 years, possibly with fines.

It is worth mentioning that some netizens had encouraged others to bring flowers to Causeway Bay to pay tribute to the suicide attacker, and some civilians did it. The government and the police have warned that this may make them violate national security law #27 and urged them to stop doing these. However, no one other than the 4 in the student union who publicly publish their praise for the suicide attack in their magazine had been arrested.

Here is how BBC news describes the arrest of the members of the student union. You can see that in the BBC news reporting, it disagrees it was wrong for those students to support a suicide attack in Hong Kong. It also uses a single quote to express they were charged for 'so-called' promoting terrorism. I highly doubt if the same happens in Britain, will BBC also put a single quote to call it 'so-called' promoting terrorism and 'so-called' wrong values?

https://www.bbc.com/zhongwen/trad/chinese-news-58254671

Here is some background about this particular student union. As a legacy, this student union had been proud of its extraordinary speeches in social movements for decades. Even 20 years ago, they had already been proactively escalating their movements to memorize the 1989 Beijing Students massacre in the democratic movement. I personally knew a president and a vice president of this student union at that time. They have felt that it is a glory to be a leader in social movements. They often like to say something outrageous and thus, believe it or not, their speeches do not represent a normal standard that Hongkongers agree.

So, based on the laws, if one praises or encourages suicide attacks, or encourage others to ask foreign to impose sanctions against the Hong Kong/Chinese government, or encourage others to attempt to subvert China's sovereign over Hong Kong, then he/she can be arrested under the national security law. However, if one just says the bad of or even defame the Hong Kong/Chinese government and make people hate these governments, he/she is unlikely to get jailed under the new national security law.

N10. Conclusion – National security law

To conclude from the above different cases, those who take passive roles, non-decision-making and at a small scale in crimes under national security law are unlikely to be charged, at least, as of now. To be more secure, avoid supporting Hong Kong independence, funding anti-government movements and organizations and avoid requesting foreign sanctions against the Chinese and the Hong Kong government.

Without sufficient evidence and a high chance of prosecution, the police have been reluctant to take action to arrest the concerned people. They usually take months after the incident to analyse whether the concerned parties have really violated the law and the chance of conviction. Looking at recent cases, some of the organizations that deemed themselves to have violated the law decommission themselves before the police start arresting their staff. Examples are the Civil Human Rights Front and the 621 Humanitarian Relief Fund. (These organizations call themselves 'Human Rights' or 'Humanitarian' but have been doing vast anti-government works and have a lot of donation scandals.)

However, the police had emphasized that decommissioning these organizations would not save the concerned individuals in the crimes from prosecution.

The above analysis is based on current cases and current national security. The Chinese and Hong Kong government may possibly change the law or their usual practices, though not likely to be a vast change unless Hong Kong's situation changes a lot.

1 month after the new national security law was in effect in 2020, I had interviewed a best friend of mine in Hong Kong. Asking her whether she supported the new national security law or not, she said, 'Well ... am ... Actually, I support the new national security law. Foreign countries have their national security laws too. Why can't only Hong Kong have its national security law? Furthermore, the law has been in effect for more than a month now. But the people are still confronting the government in streets.'

'To us who has no plan to insult our government, why should we fear the new national security law? We do the right things. We won't possibly get arrested for the new national security.'

When I wrote book 1 of this series in 2020, you could see I was not that happy about the new national security law as it would, to a certain extent, reduce the freedom of Hong Kong people. But now, seeing so much ridiculous violence even after the national security law was in effect, now I do support the new national security law. At least, it brings Hong Kong to some order again and brings the place back to some normality.

'What shall we say, then? Is the law sinful? Certainly not! Nevertheless, I would not have known what sin was had it not been for the law.'

-- Romans 7:7

N11. Other topics: National Anthem Ordinance

There is also a new National Anthem Ordinance, which was only in effect slightly earlier than the national security law, since June 2020. Obviously, one should never insult a country's national anthem and national flags, no matter which country he/she is in. These are illegal in many countries. The maximum penalty for National Anthem Ordinance in Hong Kong is HKD 50,000 (USD 6,400) and 3 years' imprisonment.

What about the national flag? Can you insult the Chinese national flag in Hong Kong? There is a case that a locally famous pro-democracy activist had insulted a Chinese national flag in Hong Kong. Together with his charge of illegal assembly, he was jailed for 4 months. The judge said that there has been no guideline on the length of the sentence in regard to insulting the Chinese national flag. The sentence was determined based on whether or not he did it publicly, whether or not he was premeditated and whether or not he encouraged other people in the scene to do the same.

https://www.hk01.com/%E7%A4%BE%E6%9C%83%E6%96%B0%E8%81%9E/567441/%E9%8D%BE%E7%BF%B0%E6%9E%97%E6%8B%8B%E5%9C%8B%E6%97%97%E5%9B%9A4%E6%9C%88-%E6%B1%82%E6%83%85%E6%8F%AD%E4%B8%8D%E5%BF%AB%E7%AB%A5%E5%B9%B4-%E7%85%A7%E9%A1%A7%E6%99%BA%E9%9A%9C%E5%BC%9F%E6%80%95%E7%B4%AF%E6%AF%8D%E7%8D%A8%E8%87%AA%E7%94%9F%E6%B4%BB

And is it legal to wave the Hong Kong British colony flag? To be honest, I do not know and do not bother to investigate this topic. In many countries, these are illegal. Just do not do it!

Hong Kong human rights, democracy, independence, Hong Kong history... All you need to know

Hong Kong Protest Leaders - Sick Facts that Western Countries do not know 2

Q1. Hong Kong ancient history; Today's composition of Hongkongers

Hong Kong has been a part of China since the Qin dynasty in 214 BC. In 204 BC, it was taken by South Vietnam and was taken by China again in the Western Han dynasty since 112 AD.

https://zh.m.wikipedia.org/wiki/%E9%A6%99%E6%B8%AF%E6%AD%B7%E5%8F%B2

In the Opium War in 1841, Hong Kong was taken by the British. It was taken by Japan for 3 years and 8 months in World War II and was returned to the British after that. The British returned Hong Kong to China in 1997. To understand why the British returned Hong Kong to China in 1997, please refer to my *book 1, Hong Kong Protest Leaders - Sick Facts that Western countries do not know.*

Cantonese, the official language of Hong Kong, was said to exist since the Qin dynasty. Cantonese has been a major language for the entire Canton area. It used to be the official language of China in at least the Tang and Song dynasties from 618 AD to 1279 AD. Hong Kong was just a small region in the Canton area. According to textbooks I studied in primary school when Hong Kong was a British colony, Hong Kong belongs to the 'Canton province' of China.

The last emperor in the Song dynasty lived in Hong Kong before he died there in 1279.

Hong Kong was only a fishing village when the British took over it in 1841.

In the time of Hong Kong as a British colony, when TV news said 'Chinese nationals', they referred to the majority race in Hong Kong, those with black hair and black eyes. 'Chinese nationals' at that time refers to those who are not British, not foreigners, etc ...

Today, the vast majority of Hongkongers are descendants of mainland Chinese who migrated to Hong Kong in the last 180 years, if not themselves comes from mainland China. Celebrities born in China includes singers Leon Lai, Faye Wong, pro-democracy activist Nathan Law and tycoon Lee Kar Shing. Hong Kong locals of mixed races are rare – the vast majority are Chinese descendants. Those with no Chinese ancestors at all exist but are very rare.

Many Hongkongers today have married Chinese spouses too. Examples are tycoon Kenneth Fok Kai-kong and former Financial Secretary of the Hong Kong government Antony Leung Kam Chung, who married Olympic gold medalists in diving Guo Jingjing and Fu Mingxia respectively. Other examples include actresses Ada Choi and Sonija Kwok. A large number of civilians married Chinese spouses too. At least 3 of my Hong Kong ex-colleagues and 20% of my married relatives in Hong Kong have Chinese Spouses.

We had analysed practical big problems with Hong Kong in my *book 1, Hong Kong Protest Leaders - Sick Facts that Western countries do not know*. In fact, family breakdown alone would already be a disaster should Hong Kong becomes independent.

Furthermore, Hong Kong people are not considered as a minority group in China. Minority groups are Uyghur, Tibetan, Mongol, Miao, etc ... Hong Kong people are officially Han, the largest ethnic group in China and the same race as many leaders in Beijing.

Many Hong Kong people recognize themselves as Chinese, due to the long history Hong Kong has been a part of China.

A celebrity spoke out, 'In the time as a British colony, the British were our master. This land belonged to the British, not us Hong Kong locals. Now, under one country two systems, we Hong Kong locals are the master of this land!'

True, when I was a teenager, as a Hong Kong local, I could tell the British were our master. Not only the governor must be a British man appointed by the British and Hongkongers have no say, but also many major decisions and senior levels of the society belonged to the British. Many things were not our say, but we just accepted it. Even music instrument examinations were under the British examination systems, and examiners were the British, not we Hong Kong locals.

Since Hong Kong has returned to China, we had the vote for our senators as we did as the British colonised Hong Kong. The Chief Executive, equivalent to the governor, must be a Hong Kong local. Despite the fact that we all believe that China has control over who eventually becomes the Chief Executive, at least, he/she must be a Hong Kong local. (For details on how the Chief Executive has been elected, please refer to my book 1, *Hong Kong Protest Leaders - Sick Facts that Western countries do not know.*)

In these 20+ years, when Hong Kong people cried, 'No national education.' Then China revoked national education. In fact, Basic Law #23 about national security had long been under discussion (argues) for 20 years, which had not been implemented because the people were not happy about it. Things only got worsen since 2019 when so many were crying for independence and protests became riots. Then China imposed new national security law to fulfil Basic Law #23.

In the first 100 years as a British colony, Hong Kong locals were not happy about the reign of the British too, until the 1970s and later. You can see this in many movies about the early years of colonization of Hong Kong, the locals generally disliked the British and the government. Same as today, in the first 30 years when China just takes over Hong Kong, it is not surprising some locals dislike China and the government. Because we are humans. Humans easily get unsatisfied with what we have, until we are about to lose them.

Q2. Chinese History in Hong Kong History

When I studied lower high school in the British Colony Hong Kong, Chinese history was a compulsory subject in all lower high schools. However, in 2013, 16 years after Hong Kong returned to China, the Chinese history subject was taken off from the menu and was incorporated into the subject of 'general knowledge'.

Perhaps, Hong Kong people feared to forget they were Chinese when they were governed by the British; and they now fear becoming the same as mainland Chinese after returning to China. It is because Hong Kong people had long been considered more superior than mainland Chinese – we were like nobles. Today, some still wish that they will continue to be nobles.

Famous thinker, Gong Zizhen (1792-1841) had a proverb, 'To perish a country, first perish its history.' Many leaders in the education sector suggest that the removal of the Chinese History subject from the high school curriculum was the reason why Hong Kong youngsters today do not know or do not recognise themselves as Chinese. The youngsters have little knowledge about their ancestors, which makes them feel no connection with the Chinese race. Chinese history used to be a very interesting topic in TV games in my childhood in the British Colony Hong Kong and is still an important topic in TV dramas today.

Some scholars also suggest that the study of a country's history is good training for students as it shows them how things develop over thousands of years. In some years, the kingdom is stronger; in other years, the kingdom becomes weak. The study of history helps students think about how incidents that happened hundreds of years ago can impact later days. Without such training, students are not trained to analyse the interrelations of incidents and remain superficial. They easily get angry when they see inciting subjects in newspapers without thinking about the causes or backgrounds of incidents thoroughly.

In 2018, Chief Executive Carrie Lam re-instated Chinese History as an independent and compulsory subject in the high school curriculum.

Q3. Anti-protest voices from the Hong Kong community

Some foreign press has been reporting as if the entire Hong Kong was supporting the democratic movements. However, in fact, many are objecting. On Youtube alone, there are not only local politicians speaking against the democratic movements, even civilians and civilian groups are speaking out against the democratic movement. Examples in Youtube channels are HKGpao, Speakout Hong Kong, Silence majority HK and many others. As explained in book 1, many Hong Kong locals feel that the democratic movement is even more undemocratic than the Hong Kong government under the communists' reign.

In 2019, there were interviews with celebrities on whether they supported the democratic movements or supported the police and the government. In their findings, only about 50% of celebrities interviewed supported the democratic movements, the remaining 50% are against it. Of course, it can be related to how the researcher sample the interviewees.

Many who previously studied abroad or previously live in a foreign country also decide to support the Chinese and the Hong Kong government. One of my favourite young pro-government politicians explained why she joined a pro-government party instead of a pro-democracy one. She said, 'Nowadays, many politicians make everything political, without focusing on how to improve the lives and welfare of the people.'

Some older generations describe the protest leaders as 'objecting against the government for the sake of objecting'. No matter what the government do, they are objecting anyway.

Refer to my book 1, chapter 2, on why so many Democrats were disqualified from their positions as lawmakers in Hong Kong. Even the Hong Kong government give them democracy and the opportunities to represent the people in the Legislative Council and other government offices, they just hate the communists no matter how.

Q4. Learn about your country – in China, Australia, the United Kingdom or Afghanistan?

In these 20 years, I have frequently heard friends and relatives in Hong Kong complaining about how pathetic people in China are. In their opinion, Chinese people generally dislike staying in China. Some Hongkongers say China is a terrible country that everyone wants to flee from. Some also felt that the Chinese are wealthy but selfish.

However, when I worked in a few top cities in China for a few months, I found that many people were living happily in China. They even suggested that I should migrate from Hong Kong to China because they feel they are living better than the Hongkongers.

Some Hong Kong people also laugh at the Chinese for not knowing they are living under limited press freedom because they are 'brainwashed' by the national education. But in my journeys, I found that the Chinese in China are not as stupid – they know they are living under press freedom and Internet censorship.

When I moved to Australia, I became even more appreciative of the Chinese people. Sometimes the Chinese helped me as they feel that Hongkongers are their kind – they have accepted us. I also knew a lot of Chinese who stay as Australian permanent residents without becoming Australian citizens because they do not want to give up their Chinese citizenship. They keep their Chinese citizenship for business advantages, travelling convenience or other reasons. Chinese people are different from what I heard of when I was in Hong Kong.

At least a few young pro-government Hong Kong politicians who frequently speak out to support the Hong Kong/Chinese governments have previously studied in the United Kingdom or other Western countries. When we learn more about other countries and compare them with our country, we found that our government is not that bad. You do not need to agree with us, but it is our opinion.

It is time we open our eyes to learn about our country.

I felt accepted when I was asked to get national education about Australia when I applied for citizenship – it was an honour for me to be invited by my new country, Australia, to learn about the nation. In contrast, sadly, in 2012 (and probably until today), Joshua Wong and other Hong Kong activists opposed national education about China for fear they would be 'brainwashed' and blindly support the communists.

Now, with no national education at all in Hong Kong, youngsters are 'brainwashed' by the anti-communist politicians who receive much more donations when the conflicts between the people and the government stir up.

Some protest leaders just considered communism the opposite of democracy. Therefore, they suggest anti-communism is equivalent to democracy and thus righteous. As you can see in book 1, some 'pro-democracy' politicians just oppose the government no matter what the government give them. Even when they were given the chance to represent the people to speak and vote in the government as senators, they are still against the government. They oppose the government for the sake of opposing because they dislike the communists even when the government was willing to cooperate.

Perhaps the 2019-20 riots, or almost civil wars, could have been avoided if Hong Kong students could have learnt more about their new country, China, that they belong to.

Talking about the United Kingdom, while we are thankful for their accepting those who wish to leave Hong Kong and begin their new lives, many decided to return to Hong Kong after living there for few months – it is never easy to migrate to another country as the culture, language and relationship networks are different. Some have learnt that Hong Kong is not as bad after living in the United Kingdom or other Western countries for months or years and decided to return.

Luckily, the publicly recognized 'evil communist government' have opened its door and allows Hong Kong people to freely leave their country as they wish, in contrast to the Taliban in Afghanistan who do not allow many to leave. From mid-2020 to mid-2021, about 90,000 Hong Kong people have migrated to other countries. And when some of these Hong Kong immigrants in the United Kingdom or other countries regret and wish to come back, the Hong Kong government again opens its door for them to come back freely whenever they want. It is how much the Hong Kong government has 'violated human rights'.

In the same period, even Australia, which condemns the Hong Kong government for its human rights situation, has forbidden its own citizens from leaving its country due to COVID-19 concerns. Each country does have its reasons to impose new rules at some point. Perhaps it is good to understand each other.

Q5. Independency and Water

Since I was in primary school, other children and I wished Hong Kong could become independent. But our teachers said, 'No, that's impossible! Because we Hong Kong do not have sufficient water supply.'

In the 1800s, soon after Hong Kong became a British colony, Hong Kong people had been facing frequent water restrictions. Hong Kong had since been building new reservoirs, but the water supply had never been sufficient.

In 1963, Hong Kong people were only given water 4 hours every 4 days in the worst water restrictions. Since then, the British colony Hong Kong started buying water from China, with increasing volume along the time. In the 1980s, Hong Kong's water supply problem was completely resolved.

https://www.hk01.com/%E7%A4%BE%E5%8D%80%E5%B0%88%E9%A1%8C/98327/%E9%A6%99%E6%B8%AF%E6%B0%B4%E8%B2%B4-%E6%B8%AF%E4%BA%BA%E7%82%BA%E6%B0%B4%E6%8E%99%E6%89%8E%E7%9A%84%E6%97%A5%E5%AD%90

https://www.hk01.com/%E7%A4%BE%E5%8D%80%E5%B0%88%E9%A1%8C/193535/50%E5%B9%B4%E4%B8%80%E9%81%87%E5%A4%A7%E6%97%B1-%E9%A6%99%E6%B8%AF%E4%B9%BE%E6%97%B1%E7%A0%B4%E6%AD%B7%E5%B9%B4%E8%A8%98%E9%8C%84-%E6%B5%AA%E8%B2%BB%E9%A3%9F%E6%B0%B4%E6%9B%BE%E8%A6%81%E7%BD%B0%E9%8C%A2%E5%9D%90%E7%9B%A3

However, in recent years, many Hong Kong politicians and critics have been telling the people that desalination is a cheaper and completely clean option and Hong Kong can now stop relying on China for their water supply. They were even able to show some data from the Middle East, proving how cheap desalination is.

Being in Australia, I would wish what they say is true. Despite the wealth and technology Australia has, the people still occasionally face water restrictions of various levels. At some time, watering your garden or washing your car can attract police to your home. The public is told to report neighbours branching these rules in the time of water restrictions.

An example is Singapore. Singapore has many similarities to Hong Kong. It is also a financial hub, a small piece of land with a huge population. It was once a part of Malaysia and is right next to it, and even today after going independent, its water supply still partially relies on Malaysia. I used to live in Singapore for quite a few months. A taxi driver said to me, 'We once heavily rely on Malaysia's water supply. For this, we feared Malaysia. But now we are much better! We now have recycled water. We can rely on Malaysia less.'

Even today, Singapore is still having a water agreement with Malaysia at least until 2061. Recycled water contributed to about 40% of Singapore's water need and is planned to continue to increase. Desalinated water is only 30% of Singapore's water need in 2019 and is expected to stay at 30% until 2061 – not as cheap or as practical as what Hong Kong pro-independence politicians have said.

https://www.mfa.gov.sg/SINGAPORES-FOREIGN-POLICY/Key-Issues/Water-Agreements

https://edition.cnn.com/2014/09/23/living/newater-singapore/index.html

https://en.wikipedia.org/wiki/Water_supply_and_sanitation_in_Singapore

To be honest, I do not think Hong Kong people will accept recycled water, at least, it is not the deal that pro-independent politicians had told them. Recycled water is not yet accepted in Hong Kong's culture. At least, the Hong Kong community has not been educated much about recycled water and cannot accept the concept of drinking the water which was once in the toilet bowl.

And it would not be as clean as the fresh water that China has been providing. According to Singaporeans who spoke to me, recycled water is more for washing rather than drinking, not something for all purposes.

Why have the findings from pro-independence politicians can illustrate cheap desalination? The Middle East, like Saudi Arabia, is the world's largest oil producer. Their energy costs can be much cheaper than most of the countries in the world. If you use the same amount of energy for desalination in Hong Kong, it will be far more expensive.

So, why do the Hong Kong pro-independence politicians and critics quote the Middle East data, which does not apply to a non-oil producer like Hong Kong? Because they are not speaking for the good of the people. They use their knowledge to deceive civilians to gain their support for independence, hoping to secure their position as Prime minister or similar in a new, independent Hong Kong. At least, gain more donations for their anti-government movements when the public believes Hong Kong can go independent.

It is not the only time the pro-independence politicians use real but inapplicable findings to mislead the Hong Kong people. In the 2019 protests, my former teacher in Hong Kong showed me some 'data' she saw in the newspaper, saying China was receiving a huge amount of money via Hong Kong. The findings were to illustrate to the public how China has been taking financial benefits from Hong Kong.

However, if you know a little bit about China's finance in the 1980s and later, China's economy has surged since the 1980s before Hong Kong returned to China in 1997. When Hong Kong returned to China, many Hong Kong civilians had been thinking of how to gain money from the increasingly wealthy China. The 'data' above, showing money were transferred into China via Hong Kong is probably just a transfer of money, using Hong Kong as the middle person due to its low tax rate and transparent regulations, such as higher transfer limits. So, Hong Kong is not the reason for China's gaining money. Instead, because foreign investors want to get

money into China, so Hong Kong was benefited by gaining fees as the middle person.

Another example, in recent years, many of my Hong Kong friends and relatives have been frequently complaining against the Hong Kong government for wasting taxpayers' money – these are what the anti-government critics told them. But most of them do not know Hong Kong has been receiving almost the lowest tax rates amongst developed countries in the world. Hong Kong people have been paying much lower tax rates than mainland Chinese too. (Refer to my book 1, *Hong Kong Protest Leaders - Sick Facts that Western countries do not know*).

Another case: In my book 1, you have watched a video of a Hong Kong local man who was set on fire for speaking against the democratic movement. Instantly, some said that there was 'solid evidence' that the man had received money to fake his being set fire on, using fake fire in TV dramas. Some even say they personally knew the man who pretended to be set on fire. However, soon, the largest hospital in the area spoke out to confirm admitting a man seriously burnt on the day. So, who said there was 'solid evidence' the incident was fake? Why did some say they personally knew the man who was 'fakely' burnt? Why did they lie? They lie to the public only want the 'democratic' movements to gain support no matter if it is right or wrong, and no matter what damages it has been causing.

Pro-independence newspapers and anti-government critics play a vital role to bring the people against the government. They often manipulate partial facts to make people angry about the government to secure their 'pro-democracy' or anti-government donations. Unfortunately, before the imposing of the new national security law in 2020, they were completely legal. These people use their knowledge and techniques not to help the community, but to deceive the community to bring them to what they want to achieve.

Older generations in Hong Kong suggest that this anti-government movement is due to youngsters' being too lucky and take everything for granted: unlimited supply of water, low tax rates, no one needs to join the army, no threat of wars, wealthy city with easy access to goods all over the world and easy job opportunities. These are what Hong Kong people have been enjoying since the 1980s. Youngsters have been given all these since they were born and have no idea they have been the lucky ones.

Q6. Proposal of implementation of one man, one vote in Hong Kong

CY Leung at his time as the Chief Executive of Hong Kong had attempted to create solid plans to implement one man one vote in the next 2017 Chief Executive Election in Hong Kong. The proposal was rejected by the Legislative Council, which was composed of Democrats, pro-China senators and independent senators.

The Democrats in the Legislative Council may not yet have successfully rejected the Federal Budget as planned in step 5 and 7 of the '10 steps to die/lose together 攬炒十步'. However, it did take away Hong Kong people's privilege of one man, one vote, at least for a few years.

According to the below websites, on August 31, 2014, the Chinese government has passed a motion to limit eligibility for the candidates in Hong Kong Chief Executive election. It was why many Hong Kong people felt that even with 'one man, one vote', all available options would be limited by China and it would be fake democracy.

Some of the Hong Kong people would like to fight for their right to determine the eligibility of candidates. However, all in all, Hong Kong is a part of China. If Hong Kong citizens can fully control all their elections, then effectively, it becomes independent. At least, in entire China, there has not been one man, one vote in any other states event at all. The privilege to vote for people's representatives in the Legislative Council and regions was exclusively given to Hong Kong people, but some of them are still not satisfied.

The decision by China on August 31, 2014, had led to the Umbrella Movement in the same year.

https://zh.m.wikipedia.org/wiki/2016%E5%B9%B4%E5%8F%8A2017%E5%B9%B4%E9%A6%99%E6%B8%AF%E6%94%BF%E6%B2%BB%E5%88%B6%E5%BA%A6%E6%94%B9%E9%9D%A9

The Democrats in the Legislative Council had not yet got a chance to reject the Federal Budget as per Benny Tai's '10 steps to die/lose together'. But they had rejected 2 out of 3 political reforms, including the proposal of 'one man, one vote' in the 2017 Chief Executive election.

https://news.rthk.hk/rthk/ch/component/k2/1580000-20210311.htm

Q7. From 1989 Tiananmen Square to the 2014 Umbrella movement and 2019 protests

In the 1989 Tiananmen Square Massacre, Hong Kong people and most of the world were impressed by the bravery and passion of those Beijing students. The Western world also condemned China for killing the students who only fought for democracy.

The Beijing 1989 student pro-democracy movement had a profound impact on Hong Kong. On the one hand, some decided to migrate to foreign countries for fear that the same will happen to Hong Kong after the British colony returns to China in 1997. On the other hand, those who decided to stay in Hong Kong always remember how dangerously and how terribly China can treat its people.

Every year June 4, Hong Kong citizens have been holding the Tiananmen vigil in Victoria Park. In the last 3 decades, every year, tens of thousands of Hong Kong people attend the vigil. When I was a kid, my parents had an oversized book, *The tragically magnificent democratic movement*, which was a collection of photos of the massacre, especially the bloody ones. The cover of that book was the photo of the iconic Goddess of Democracy, with a black background. The front cover of my book series was inspired by that book.

Since then, many Hong Kong politicians have named their political parties with the word 'democracy' or 'democratic'. When I was a young adult in Hong Kong, I did vote for some of the politicians as they call themselves 'Democrats'. However, does the name reflect what they actually do? Are Liberal and Labour not democratic because they do not have the word 'democracy' in their party names?

In the recent 20 years, Hong Kong politicians use the word 'democracy' even more either to gain votes in elections or gain financial donations. Many people also try to copy from those Beijing students in 1989.

Joshua Wong presents himself as a 'scholar' because, in 1989, many supported the Beijing top students (scholars) as they were considered more well-educated and advantageous over the general public. They were considered leaders of society. Joshua Wong presents himself as a 'scholar' in front of foreigners, which he is clearly not one in the eyes of Hong Kong people. That was why he called his political party 'learning civilians 學民' in the Hong Kong language and intentionally wrongly translated it as 'Scholarism 學者' to gain international supports.

He also copied the hunger strike from 1989 Beijing students, though his hunger strike was fake. (For both topics, refer to my book 1, *Hong Kong Protest Leaders - Sick Facts that Western countries do not know.*)

Surprisingly, many foreigners believe Joshua Wong is a pioneer of Hong Kong democratic movements. Many of his slogans and justifications are just direct copies from 1989 Beijing students.

'Peaceful protest', 'unarmed protesters' and 'a fight for a beautiful value, democracy' were all major justifications directly copied from the 1989 Beijing pro-democracy movement.

2014 Umbrella Movement (Occupy Movement) was a huge mistake. At that time, the protests were largely peaceful. Hong Kong people even prided themselves on (actually, the organising politicians told them they should pride themselves on) the super peaceful large-scale protests, considering the enormous number of protesters. My close relatives in Hong Kong said, 'Foreigners are surprised by our super peaceful protests'. And I said, 'Most of the violent protests in the world start with peaceful protests.'

The protests praises 'unlawful righteousness 違法達義' and 'civil disobedience 公民抗命'. At that time, older generations and some local critics have blamed the Umbrella Movement for 'poisoning people's hearts' by advocating doing unlawful things for what one believes to be right. In the 2014 Umbrella Movement (Occupy Movement), protesters illegally occupied streets in central districts of Hong Kong, paralysing transports, top-tier businesses, schools and government organizations in the area.

Some also blamed the protest leaders for blackmailing the government to agree on what they want by threatening to harm the livelihoods or other welfares of other Hongkongers who do not agree to the movement. Some pro-civilian politicians have pointed out that 'civil disobedience' is supposed to be sacrificing activists' own interests, rather than sacrificing other locals' interests. Examples were Mahatma Gandhi and Nelson Rolihlahla Mandela.

In 2019 protests, Hong Kong protesters continued to justify themselves with 'unlawful righteousness 違法達義' and 'civil disobedience 公民抗命'. When many were wearing helmets and throwing bricks towards the police and pro-China civilians, they continued to emphasize they are 'peaceful' and 'unarmed protesters'. In earlier stages of the protests, Democrats simply deny the accusations of physical attacks and damages of properties by protesters, saying those were policemen disguising protesters by wearing masks and black clothes like them. But later, more evidence was captured on cameras and some youngsters pleaded guilty in courts. Examples were anti-government civilians setting fire on a pro-China Hong Kong local (refer to book 1) and students preparing weapons in their university and practising throwing petrol bombs in their university campus. The Democrats still insisted protesters were 'largely peaceful' though they could no longer declare (completely) 'peaceful'.

Pro-protest civilians generally say they feel that the Beijing democratic movement has repeated in Hong Kong. But pro-government and anti-protest civilians feel they are very different - students in Beijing democratic movements were real heroes, while those in Hong Kong protests were just attempted copies by using 'democracy' and 'peaceful protests' as slogans. But the nature of protests is completely different.

Even in Benny Tai's '10 steps to die/lose together 攬炒十步', his steps 9 and 10 refer to repeating the 1989 Beijing Tiananmen Square Massacre in Hong Kong. It was unambiguous and both pro-government and pro-protest civilians agree it was what Benny Tai meant. 'Step 9 ... Suppression (by the government) turns very bloody ... Step 10 ... Western countries will impose sanctions on the Chinese Communist financially and politically' - These were exactly what happened in the 1989 Beijing Tiananmen Square Massacre. And Benny Tai wanted to (warned to) repeated these in Hong Kong.

Luckily, the Chinese government had changed a lot over the last 30 years. At least, the people in their leadership team had changed and the way they deal with things have changed. Benny Tai and those self-proclaimed Democrats successfully acted on most steps in his 10 steps to die/lose together. However, the Chinese government had not copied the massacre from 1989 Beijing to 2020 Hong Kong as Benny Tai had planned. The Chinese government had learnt from their mistake in 1989's massacre and did not do it again. It just does not confess.

Finally, 'foreign governments' sanctions against the Chinese government' is also the idea copied from the 1989 Tiananmen Square democratic movement. The difference is that, in 1989, foreign sanctions were the natural results of the massacre. But in 2019-20 protests, pro-democracy politicians and their supporters proactively approach foreign governments to impose sanctions against China.

From 2014 protests, an increasing number of Hongkongers have become less supportive of 1989 Beijing students. Some started feeling that the Beijing democratic movements had set a bad example to copy from in the Hong Kong protests. Now, some Hongkongers realize that if Beijing had not stopped the democratic movements in 1989, it would have ended up with the chaos and riots that we saw in 2019-20's Hong Kong protests.

In 2021, the Hong Kong government used COVID-19 as an excuse to forbid the people from attending the yearly Tiananmen vigil in Victoria Park. Will there still be Tiananmen vigils in coming years after COVID-19? I do not know. I do appreciate the students sacrificed in 1989 and see them as heroes. But if the price of the vigil is the violence and social disorders we saw in the Hong Kong society in 2019-21, then I would rather stop the vigil too.

Q8. Human rights in Hong Kong?

According to the reputable Fraser Institute in Canada, Hong Kong has the 3rd best human rights index from 2018 to 2020 amongst the 162 countries it researched. In 2020's report, it stated, 'The HFI also finds a strong relationship between human freedom and democracy. Hong Kong is an outlier in this regard. Although Hong Kong's ratings and rankings have decreased since 2008, the impact of the Chinese Communist Party's unprecedented interventions in the territory in 2019 and 2020 are not reflected in this year's report'.

The research had not taken into account the new national security law.

https://www.fraserinstitute.org/studies/human-freedom-index-2018

https://www.fraserinstitute.org/studies/human-freedom-index-2019

https://www.fraserinstitute.org/studies/human-freedom-index-2020

That means before the 2019-20 Hong Kong pro-democracy movement, human rights issues which the Democrats had been accusing their government of was not that justified under international standards.

In 2016, the Cato Institute in Washington, D.C. even found Hong Kong the best human freedom in the world in their studies. It was when Joshua Wong and other so-called Democrats were asking the United States to look into Hong Kong's human rights problems:

https://www.cato.org/sites/cato.org/files/human-freedom-index-files/human-freedom-index-2016.pdf

As such, many Hong Kong anti-protest locals laughed at protesters who asked the United States to help to combat Hong Kong's human rights issues – the United States has been having much lower rankings (#17) in the human freedom index than Hong Kong (#3) for all those years!

https://www.speakout.hk/%E6%B8%AF%E4%BA%BA%E8%8A%B1%E7%94%9F/48557/-%E7%B6%B2%E7%B5%A1%E7%86%B1%E8%A9%B1-%E4%BA%BA%E9%A1%9E%E8%87%AA%E7%94%B1%E6%8C%87%E6%95%B8-%E9%A6%99%E6%B8%AF%E6%8E%92%E7%AC%AC3-%E7%A4%BA%E5%A8%81%E8%80%85%E5%90%91%E6%8E%9217%E7%9A%84%E7%BE%8E%E5%9C%8B-%E6%B1%82%E5%8A%A9-#selected

For this, along with alleged fundings from the United States for Hong Kong's democracy movement, there has long been rumours that Hong Kong pro-democracy leaders have been receiving the money to incite the riots.

Hong Kong Protest Leaders – Sick Facts that Western Countries do not know 2

Many Hong Kong pro-protest locals have a misunderstanding of what western countries mean by human rights, after being brainwashed by pro-democracy newspapers and critics like Apple Daily.

In Chinese New Year 2021, I talked to a group of my close relatives in Hong Kong. Talking about the topic of lock-down in Australia, my relative asked, 'How does the Australian police know the address of the people that they investigate?' I said, 'Check their driver's license or photo ID. The person's home address is there.' My relatives were surprised, 'What??? How would the police have this right to read these?' I said, 'Of course the police have such power!' I was astonished that today's Hong Kong people are expecting police not to have the power to examine anything basic due to human rights or privacy protections.

In order to add fire to the conflicts and disagreement between the people and the Hong Kong government and police, Hong Kong protest leaders often educate the public to fight for unrealistic rights that even Western countries would not normally grant to their people. Look at the girl with a ruptured eye's debate on her medical records. Look at Joshua Wong's anger about the police's reading his mobile phone data on his arrest. They are telling the public that police should not have the authority to check any of these even on suspects of criminal offences. Unfortunately, some civilians and youngsters who do not know the usual international standard become convinced that human rights mean doing whatever they want and having whatever rights they wish to.

Sadly, many foreign countries blindly support this so-called Hong Kong democratic movement, without the chance to understand the details of the so-called human rights or democracy these protest leaders are fighting for. It is partially because Hong Kong Democrats sometimes intentionally mistranslate their slogans and their complaints, or chop off the immoral and illegal parts of their demands when they present their stories to Western countries. Chinese speaking countries like Singapore is less supportive of this so-called democratic movement because they can read the language and know what was actually happening.

Many foreign newspapers say that Hong Kong protest activists were jailed for 'unauthorized assembly' instead of 'illegal assembly', accusing the Chinese government of violating Hong Kong Basic Law which guarantees the right to peaceful assembly. However, in fact, 'illegal assembly' has always been a usual charge in Hong Kong even when it was a British colony. You can easily hear of this charge in Hong Kong Movies even produced before Hong Kong returned to China.

https://www.npr.org/2021/04/01/983346689/hong-kongs-jimmy-lai-6-others-found-guilty-for-roles-in-pro-democracy-protests

Most of the foreign press emphasizes Hong Kong protest leaders were arrested for 'peaceful protests'. Even in Australia, some were arrested for 'peaceful' anti-mask protests or arrested for going for sunbath under COVID-19 lockdown. Yes, COVID-19 is a global epidemic. But is it the only acceptable reason to criminalise peaceful protests? Can't a government make its decision based on its situation too? Even in the most democratic countries, sometimes it is reasonable to arrest those in peaceful protests when the government has given orders on what the public must do or must not do.

In a case about a Hong Kong protest at court, the jury had said, 'in such atmosphere and recent anger and emotions of the people, it is barely impossible to expect peaceful protests. It was merely lucky to have only a few people injured and no one was seriously injured.' And it was why illegal assembly was bringing more problems than one may reckon.

When Hong Kong protesters hear so many Western countries are backing them, they become even more convinced they are justified to break the laws.

So, if you really want to support Hong Kong people, please, say NO to the so-call democratic movements.

A Chinese scholar said, 'If a foreign government supports the Hong Kong so-called pro-democracy movements, let Nathan Law and others do the same in your country.'

Q9. Democracy in Hong Kong?

As you can see, before the 2014 Umbrella Movement (Occupy Movement), Hong Kong people have been given most of the democracy. All of us had a vote of who represent us in the Legislative Council. We were also granted one man one vote for the Chief Executive of Hong Kong. The only thing Hong Kong people did not have was full control of candidates for the Chief Executive.

Compared to mainland China, citizens did not and do not have any of these.

In the 2014 democratic movement, protesters demanded to gain full control of candidates for the Chief Executive. This had not been granted as a result of the movement.

In the 2019 democratic movements, originally, protesters' only demand to stop the legislation of extradition bill with China, which was finally granted. However, the price was the large number of people engaging in illegal activities, damaged economy, bombs, civilians attacking each other for different political views, vastly worsened relationship with China and the new national security laws reducing people's freedoms.

Isn't it much worse than the extradition bill? Why must we go on this path?

As a result of the 2019-20 democratic movements, China had decided to impose 'patriots only' elections for the position of Chief Executive. While Western countries generally condemned this move, former Chief Executive CY Leung emphasized that 'selecting through consultations' patriot only candidates is in line with both the Sino–British Joint Declaration and Hong Kong Basic Law #45:

> 'The Chief Executive of the Hong Kong Special Administrative Region shall be selected by election or **through consultations held locally** and be appointed by the Central People's Government.'

https://www.hk01.com/%E6%B7%B1%E5%BA%A6%E5%A0%B1%E9%81%93/581083/%E5%8D%94%E5%95%86%E8%AB%96-%E7%82%BA%E4%BD%95%E6%9C%83%E8%A2%AB%E5%AF%AB%E9%80%B2-%E5%9F%BA%E6%9C%AC%E6%B3%95

Surprisingly, not everyone in Hong Kong is against this change. After experiencing the riots and chaos in the 'democratic movements', some saw the problem of democratic systems – there must be at least 2 major political parties spending a lot of efforts to confront each other and convince the people that their side is better. It also means only half of the best politicians would be in the government. With only 1 party, in contrast, all the best politicians can only join that party and can always work in the government. It also avoids the waste of resources for marketing and confronting each other.

Another advantage of the non-democratic system in China, they said, is the consistency of plans and policies. In contrast, in a democratic country like Australia, when the power goes to Liberal from Labour or vice versa, all the senior government ministers change. When it happens every 4 years, much done by the prior party can go to waste and the new political party start their new different plans from scratch. And these happen every 4 years or best, 12 years or so.

You may not agree with the above theory that they suggest. Anyway, the new system does gain a certain level of support from the locals. To many civilians, the most important is the stability, safety and prosperity of the society, not which political party is leading.

Hong Kong Protest Leaders – Sick Facts that Western Countries do not know 2

Youngsters manipulated in riots and attacks

Y1. Hong Kong police – your classmate? Or a star?

According to the website of the Hong Kong Police Force, policemen/policewomen must be permanent residents of Hong Kong and have lived there for at least 7 years. That means all policemen or policewomen should be local Hongkongers.

In 2019 protests, there was once a rumour that few Hong Kong policemen were found to speak Mandarin, alleged to be members of the Chinese army disguising as Hong Kong policemen. While this rumour was not confirmed and that speaking mandarin alone does not imply they must be Chinese nationals. It would be a real scandal if there are indeed members of the Chinese army in the Hong Kong Police Force, which is supposed to be 100% Hong Kong people.

https://www.police.gov.hk/ppp_en/15_recruit/er.html

In fact, speaking Mandarin may imply their parents speak Mandarin to them at home and they become more fluent in Mandarin than Cantonese as they grow up. It may also mean they came to Hong Kong in their childhood and thus speak more fluent Mandarin than Cantonese.

Unlike the Chinese army in the Tiananmen Square massacre who comes from all around the enormous land of China and have a relatively low education level, the Hong Kong Police Force is comprised of only local Hongkongers. They can be your relatives or your neighbours. For more senior positions, most of them have bachelor's degrees or have completed tertiary education.

One of the famous current policemen we all know is Cheng Pak Lam, a Chief Inspector of Police. He was a child actor star when he was a kid and he represented Hong Kong people to send flowers to Prince Charles and Princess Diana in their visit to Hong Kong when Cheng was 4 years old.

He was graduated from the University of Hong Kong, which is considered to be the best university there.

Our first Olympic Gold Medalist since Hong Kong returns to China, Cheung Ka Long (2021, fencing), was hated by many self-proclaimed pro-democracy Hongkongers before he won the game. Their reason was pure because his father was a policeman. Nowadays, being a policeman seems to be a sin.

Anyone around you can easily become a policeman/policewoman too. One of my university classmates from my top university had also joined the Hong Kong police force. He had never been a friend of mine and I am not sure if he is still a policeman or not today.

A relative of mine used to be a part-time policewoman in Hong Kong. It was before Hong Kong returned to China.

I do not know whether any of my other ex-classmates, ex-neighbours or ex-colleagues had joined the police force or not. And I would not be surprised. It is just a normal local occupation.

As I explained in book 1, the entire Hong Kong population are very well educated. Even junior members in the police force have studied at least high school – of course, everyone who grew up in Hong Kong must study at least high school. From the above, you can also see a lot of slightly senior Hong Kong policemen today have university degrees.

Y2. Dragon (Police) Slaying Brigade

Let us talk about the famous 'Hong Kong twelve' again. They were the twelve men who were arrested by the Chinese customs for mistakenly entering the Chinese sea when they attempted to escape to Taiwan. 4 of the 12 were members of the Dragon Slaying Brigade 屠龍小隊.

https://zh.wikipedia.org/wiki/12%E6%B8%AF%E4%BA%BA%E6%A1%88#%E8%A2%AB%E6%89%A3%E7%95%99%E8%80%85%E7%AE%80%E4%BB%8B

The name Dragon Slaying Brigade 屠龍小隊 was inspired by Hong Kong police's Special Tactical Contingent 速龍小隊. The Special Tactical Contingent is a squad specialised in quickly taking situations under control in larger incidents. For this, they often get involved in 2019-20 protests' large-scale riots and threats.

And the Dragon Slaying Brigade 屠龍小隊 was born to kill the Special Tactical Contingent 速龍小隊 or any other police officers.

https://zh.wikipedia.org/wiki/%E5%B1%A0%E9%BE%8D%E5%B0%8F%E9%9A%8A

But one does not need to join the 'Dragon Slaying Brigade' to kill police officers. Wong Fung-lam, another member in the 'Hong Kong Twelve', pleaded guilty for his attempt to set fire at the Mong Kok Police Station 旺角警署外企圖縱火 by throwing petrol bombs towards the police station on October 14, 2019. He was only 16 years old when he committed the crime.

https://www.hkcnews.com/article/43691/12%E6%B8%AF%E4%BA%BA-%E9%BB%83%E8%87%A8%E7%A6%8F-%E6%A3%84%E4%BF%9D%E6%BD%9B%E9%80%83-43692/12%E6%B8%AF%E4%BA%BA

As mentioned in Chapter N9, a man committed a suicide attack by killing himself after severely injuring a police officer that he saw on the street.

Nowadays, being a policeman/policewoman alone is sufficient to attract suicide attacks, regardless of whether one has done anything wrong or not at all. When protest leaders stir up conflicts to secure their donation incomes, police officers need to sacrifice their lives and youngsters incited to attack need to sacrifice their future in prison.

Y3. Heroism and the 'wonderful' prisons

In the Hong Kong democratic movement, protest leaders and 'pro-democracy' politicians tell the public that the police and the communists are threatening their lives and safety. They tell the public that everyone against the communists is in danger and must do anything, regardless of lawful or unlawful. They say, these are the fight for their future. It is what they call 'unlawful righteousness'. Many 'pro-democracy' politicians even **praise the beauty of imprisonment and encourage the public to get jailed.**

Former Associate Professor of Law in the University of Hong Kong, Benny Tai Yiu-ting, is a pioneer of the 'unlawful righteousness' ideology.

https://truereport.hk/2020/23/%E6%96%B0%E8%81%9E/%E6%B8%AF%E8%81%9E/4762/

In this report, **Benny Tai re-iterates the rationality of 'unlawful righteousness'** 戴耀廷 … 重申「違法達義」的合理性. Many other lawyers and law students condemned him. He responded, 'When the laws are not righteous, then the laws are not laws.' 'If the people reckon that the laws are not up to the standard of 'righteousness', then the laws should have no power to punish the people. Not only so, but the people should also have the right to violate these unrighteous laws and amend the laws and regulations so that righteousness can be achieved.' 「不公義的法律就不是法律」。「若人民認為一些法律不能符合公義的要求，法律不單沒有規範效力懲處他們，人民更有權利以違反那些不公義規則的行動，去改變法律及制度，以達成公義。」

It is how he, as a lawyer, educate youngsters to violate laws. Of course, he is always careful enough to avoid violating laws himself.

Under Hong Kong laws, it was completely legal for him to tell others to violate the laws, as long as he does not do these himself. Luckily, with the new national security law, this kind of bad teacher finally can have a long jail term - because it is now unlawful to encourage to violate the national security law.

Before the establishment of the new national security law, protest leaders like Joshua Wong and Benny Tai are often only arrested under minor charges such as illegal assembly, incitement or election fraud, which only put them behind bars for about 3 years even with multiple of these charges. In contrast, youngsters who were incited to throw petrol bombs or other weapons can be sentenced to many years even after pleading guilty.

A barrister and **Hong Kong Civic Party's former leader praises the wonder of getting criminal records**. (Refer to the last page of this book) Since then, his speech has been frequently quoted by the Hong Kong locals when they laugh at the imprisonment of these so-called 'pro-democracy' activists.

Martin Lee Chu-ming, a barrister and the founding chairman of the United Democrats of Hong Kong and Hong Kong Democratic Party, expressed that he felt **proud to be arrested** with the youngers. He said this when he went on bail under a charge of illegal assembly on August 18, 2019. He said that it was his first time to be a defendant but he did not regret what he did. He had been sad to see youngsters being arrested and he now felt 'proud' to share the same with the youngsters.

民主黨創黨主席李柱銘在離開警署時指，自己以 1000 元保釋，期間無需到警署報到，並指自己涉及去年 8 月 18 日在

維園組織及參與「未經批准集結」的遊行。… 他又指,是次是自己首次成為被告,但指並無為所作所為感到後悔。他亦指,過往看到多名青年被捕而感到過意不去,並指現在有機會與年輕人一起行走民主路感到驕傲。

https://hd.stheadline.com/news/realtime/hk/1750062/%E5%8D%B3%E6%99%82-%E6%B8%AF%E8%81%9E-%E6%9D%8E%E6%9F%B1%E9%8A%98%E7%A8%B1%E8%88%87%E9%9D%92%E5%B9%B4%E5%90%8C%E8%B5%B0%E6%B0%91%E4%B8%BB%E8%B7%AF%E6%84%9F%E9%A9%95%E5%82%B2-%E9%84%A7%E7%82%B3%E5%BC%B7-%E6%87%89%E6%84%9F%E7%BE%9E%E6%81%A5

Agnes Chow Ting said she dropped the tears of joy for being sentenced to prison. She learnt to make cakes in prison's cooking classes. (Refer to Chapter L4). This makes me think of the cooking classes in Pacific Island's resorts …

Eddie Chu Hoi-dick, a former pro-democracy senator elected by the people, said that he felt stressed going to court and felt prison like his home. According to his Facebook post on August 22, 2021, he said, '**Fellow inmates (or translate it as 'friends in prisons') sincerely feel like 'getting home' when we get to the prison car** from court. We **wish to get back to prison for dinner as early as possible and do something we love in prison**. 囚友們真是帶著「回家」的心情上囚車,希望盡快回到監獄吃飯,回到監倉內做喜歡做的事'

https://www.youtube.com/watch?v=wx-hYZk6o3A

Sounds like prisons are enjoyable places where people rush to get there to do something they love.

Agnes Chow's politician friend, Tiffany Yuen Ka-wai, prepared a book list to read and other necessary materials for going to prison. Sounds like getting prepared for a long vacation on the beach.

https://www.facebook.com/silentmajorityhk/photos/a.500993386656439/3886198554802555/

Soon, Tiffany Yuen made friends there and had a **new fight for their rights in prison**. She, along with another 5, were found to possess forbidden materials in prison. Facing punishment, **another 18 inmates threatened the prison officers to stop their punishment**. Eventually, the prison needed to send the Regional Response Teams there to put them back to order.

https://www.youtube.com/watch?v=byMOVV9mJes

Tiffany Yuen and some others had been failures in their fights in society. At least, they now can have new fights for their other rights in prison.

Benny Tai, who is in custody for his +35 election, reveals that he is learning to enjoy the present in his letter to his Hong Kong activist friend, Shiu Ka-chun. Benny Tai says that he has learnt not to rethink the past and not to predict the future. He only wants to **enjoy the present 「享受」當下 (when he is in custody)**.

https://www.singtao.ca/5192586/2021-09-05/news-%E6%88%B4%E8%80%80%E5%BB%B7%E7%8D%84%E4%B8%AD%E6%9B%B8%E4%BF%A1+%E7%A8%B1%E5%AD

%B8%E7%BF%92%E3%80%8C%E4%BA%AB%E5%8F%97%E7%95%B6%E4%B8%8B%E3%80%8D/?variant=us-eng

Jimmy Lai said that the 'peak of your life is when you were in prison' in his interview with New York times and/or his book:

https://www.aei.org/wp-content/uploads/2020/12/Natan-Sharansky-with-Jimmy-Lai-transcript.pdf?x91208

No wonder so many youngsters rush to commit crimes in the frontline and join the 'enjoyable' and 'glorious' prison lives.

Let us listen to Chris Tang Ping-keung, the Secretary for Security, about the trend of crimes amongst Hong Kong youngsters.

He said, 'First, there has been a surge in youngsters committing crimes about the anti-extradition bill protests. Amongst the 7700 people arrested, about 40% are students. Within these 40%, 60% of which are higher education or university students and the remaining 40% are high school students. There was a huge difference before and after the start of the new semester last year (i.e., around August to September 2019, just after the anti-extradition bill protests started). Before the start of the semester, there were only 25% of the arrested were students, and now it surged to 40%. Furthermore, the ratio of arresting students increased from 6% to about 26%. This is very worrying.

'For juveniles arrested under the age of 18, there was a huge difference before and after the start of the new semester last year. Especially for criminally destroying properties, those arrested under the age of 18 increased from about 5% in July 2019 to over 50% in January 2020. In recent arrests of criminally destroying properties, such as * using hammers to damages stores and their items, many of the offenders are under the age of 18. We are so worried about this trend.

'Second, the Law-abiding consciousness (of the people in the society) has become weaker and weaker. The consciousness of disobeying laws has become increasingly strong. In the fight against the extradition bill, in earlier stages, the people blocked roads and throw bricks. In the later stages, ** some burst into and damage the Legislative Council, others severely damage the public transports such as MTR and the light rail. In the last stages, they throw petrol bombs. There was also a case of *** setting fire on a living man. And some were murdered by their throwing bricks. Explosives and remote bombs were also found. These are all very worrying.

'Not only those who commit crimes are wrong but also few public figures telling the public that they are right to commit crimes. Public figures, some of which are lawyers, even tell the public that **** criminal records make one's life even more wonderful. These lawyers suggest that violence is a solution to problems! **These lawyers have no criminal records and do not commit violent crimes themselves, but when youngsters hear what they say, they would believe it is correct to murder or damage others' properties as long as they feel justified! Now the public, especially the youngsters, are losing their law-abiding consciousness.** That is super worrying – it can develop into a collapse of the law-obeying system! That means people are not obeying laws anymore! They just do whatever they consider being justified!'

https://www.youtube.com/watch?v=kIYjNYT5kCc

Here is the number he announced. Please note this URL is a pro-China website:

http://www.takungpao.com.hk/news/232109/2020/0303/421856.html

* Refer to book 1, *Hong Kong Protest Leaders - Sick Facts that Western countries do not know*. There is a video of many masked youngsters breaking into and damaging Chinese Enterprises in Hong Kong and local stores which supported the government or spoke against the pro-democracy movement.

** Refer to the documentary movie 佔領立法會 *Taking back the Legislature* in Chapter L7 to watch what protesters broke into and destroy the interiors of the government building.

*** To watch the video, refer to book 1, *Hong Kong Protest Leaders - Sick Facts that Western countries do not know*.

**** Refer to the last page of this book to see who had said these.

Youngsters manipulated in riots and attacks

Look at this 18-year-old man who admitted rioting in a violent demonstration. He was the last to leave the scene. A can of lighter fluid, a spanner, a flashlight and a broken hiking stick was found in his possession on his arrest. Many wrote to witness that he has been a good person before he joined the riot and begged the judge to reduce his sentence.

The judge said that the young man was unpremeditated and was merely one of the many protesters who responded to online calls to stage protests in the university's vicinity in a bid to scatter police officers with their numbers. The judge was convinced that he was genuinely remorseful. After the reduction of sentence for his pleading guilty and his teachers and friends' letters about his good character, he still needs to stay behind bars for 30 months.

This young man believed he was only fighting for righteousness. He believed he was only fighting for his future and his generation's future. He believed the police were evil and he came to help the protesters to confront them. But now, he was used by the protest activists to join the riots and needed to stay behind bars for 2.5 years.

https://www.scmp.com/news/hong-kong/law-and-crime/article/3147350/hong-kong-protests-student-who-admitted-rioting-during

And he was only one of the young people who had made the wrong decision in joining the riots. Many others like him, believe they are only fighting for their futures, fighting for righteousness, either lawful or unlawful. They believe the police and the government are trying to harm them, so they bring weapons to attack the evil police to support the protests.

Think about when we were young and passionate, in such atmosphere and 'teaching' in the society, we could all easily make the same mistake. And those protest leaders who incited them to riot, if not because of the new national security law, would have been at large and continue to stir up conflicts by bringing protesters to sensitive zones to ensure conflicts (Chapter L3), making up fake news (Chapter F1, F2, F3, L6) and putting on advertisement in foreign newspapers (Chapter L6). All these will secure massive donation incomes into protest leaders' pockets (Chapter L10).

Mothers of some Hong Kong youngsters ask Joshua Wong, 'You stir up people's conflicts, leaving them at the frontline to attack the police, putting them into prisons. As for yourself, you stay in the safe zone at the back. Don't you feel evil?'

Perhaps it makes one think of Joshua Wong's bringing the girl to a top 5-star hotel room when what he called his 'siblings' were arrested and suffering.

Now, with the new national security law, the so-called Hong Kong Democrats can eventually get longer jail terms. Not only some Hong Kong parents should celebrate as these Democrats can no longer incite the people, especially youngsters, to riot and get jailed. But also the Democrats themselves should celebrate as they can now feel proud to get arrested, drop the tears of joy and stay at the peak of their lives as they have said for much longer.

As these so-called Democrats loved Occupy Movement in 2014. Now, at least they can continue their movement by occupying the prisons ... Hope there are enough rooms.

Youngsters manipulated in riots and attacks

On July 1, 2021, a man has attacked a police officer and then suicide in Causeway Bay. While the majority of Hong Kong society was furious about the terrorist attack, other locals, including a mother with her young kid, brought flowers to pay tribute to this 'human right hero'.

https://www.wsj.com/articles/suicide-attack-on-hong-kong-police-officer-highlights-tension-over-chinas-rule-11625666739

A university student union also pay tribute to this suicided 'hero' in their university magazine, praising his contributions to Hong Kong. (Refer to Chapter N8)

16 days after Apple Daily closed down, on July 10, 2021, a completely naked female ex-journalist of Apple Daily attempted to burst into the Hong Kong government headquarter. Marijuana was found in her backpack. The 24-year-old woman was arrested under obscene exposure, obstructing government officer(s) and drug possession.

https://www.hk01.com/%E7%AA%81%E7%99%BC/649151/%E5%89%8D-%E8%98%8B%E6%9E%9C%E6%97%A5%E5%A0%B1-%E5%A5%B3%E8%A8%98%E8%80%85%E5%A4%9C%E9%97%96%E6%94%BF%E7%B8%BD-%E9%99%A4%E8%A1%AB%E5%90%B5%E9%AC%A7%E6%8F%AD%E8%97%8F%E5%A4%A7%E9%BA%BB%E8%A2%AB%E6%8D%95

These are where Hong Kong is now heading to. It is the 'democratic movement' that some foreign countries are today blindly supporting when they do not know the details. Now Hong Kong is no longer a colony. Hope foreign governments can give Hong Kong people a chance to decide how they wish to deal with the situation.

'Criminal records make one's life even more wonderful.'

-- Alvin Yeung Ngok-kiu

(Hong Kong Civic Party's former leader;

Former Hong Kong senator)

August 16, 2017

「留案底令人生更精彩」

-- 楊岳橋 (前公民黨黨魁; 前立法會議員)

Source:

https://evchk.wikia.org/zh/wiki/%E6%A5%8A%E5%B2%B3%E6%A9%8B#.E6.A1.88.E5.BA.95.E4.BB.A4.E4.BA.BA.E7.94.9F.E6.9B.B4.E7.B2.BE.E5.BD.A9

https://www.youtube.com/watch?v=j0laPPEx2B4

(and many more sources …)

Glossary

* **Chief Executive** - equivalent to a prime minister of a country. More accurately, it is equivalent to a governor in the British colony.

* **Sino–British Joint Declaration** – the agreement signed between the United Kingdom and China in 1985 that Hong Kong's sovereignty would be returned to China from 1-July-1997. For more background, please refer to my book 1, *Hong Kong Protest Leaders - Sick Facts that Western countries do not know*.

* **Hong Kong Basic Law** - the Basic Law was enacted under the Constitution of China to implement the Sino-British Joint Declaration. It came into effect from 1-July-1997, the date Hong Kong's sovereignty returned to China. For more details, please refer to my book 1, *Hong Kong Protest Leaders - Sick Facts that Western countries do not know*.

* **Yellow (ribbon)** – Pro-democracy people, businesses, parties or materials. This terminology has been used since the 2014 Umbrella Movement. In the latter days, the word 'ribbon' is frequently omitted.

* **Blue (ribbon)** – Pro-police or Pro-government people, businesses, parties or materials. This terminology has been used since the 2014 Umbrella Movement. In the latter days, the word 'ribbon' is frequently omitted.

* **Sibling 手足** - Hong Kong pro-democracy people call each other 'siblings' or 'righteous heroes'. This terminology has been used since the 2019 protests. The original word 'Sibling 手足' refers to brothers and sisters, or counterparts in the same gang or small organization.

www.ingramcontent.com/pod-product-compliance
Lightning Source LLC
Chambersburg PA
CBHW070713020526
44107CB00078B/2458